Classic AMERICAN

Costume Jewelry

Volume 2
IDENTIFICATION & VALUE GUIDE

JACQUELINE REHMANN

COLLECTOR BOOKS
A Division of Schroeder Publishing Co., Inc.

All cover jewelry is from the private collection of Marianna Schweitzer,
www.rubylane.com/shops/sweetiesgemz

Front, upper left: Eisenberg brooch, signed "EISENBERG ORIGINAL STERLING," 3½" x 3¼", *$600.00 – 800.00.* *Next row, left to right:* Marcel Boucher TORII gate, signed with the Phrygian cap, enamel with clear rhinestone accents, 3¼" x 2½", *$800.00 – 1,000.00.* Kenneth Jay Lane Cartier-inspired bangle with faux coral dragon heads, gold-tone setting, green cabochon accents, and a spring clasp, *$400.00 – 500.00.* Boucher Phoenix bird brooch decorated with light sapphire and chrysoprase cabochon stones with Siam and clear rhinestones, 1960s, signed "©BOUCHER" with the design number, 4¼" x 3¼", *$700.00 – 800.00.* *Bottom row, left to right:* Heron brooch features plastic inserts, enameled accents, and diamante rhinestones, attributed to Hattie Carnegie, 3" high, *$500.00 – 600.00.* Kenneth Jay Lane Maltese cross, crystal clear rhinestones and turquoise colored cabochons, signed "K.J.L.," 3½" x 3½", *$300.00 – 400.00.*

Back, top row, left to right: Elephant brooch, ivory colored plastic inserts, enameled accents, clear rhinestones, 3" x 2½", Hattie Carnegie, unsigned, *$300.00 – 400.00.* HAR brooch, enameled basket of poured glass fruit, signed "©HAR," 2" tall, *$75.00 – 125.00.* *Middle row, left to right:* Chinese lion brooch, antiqued gold-tone setting with pavé rhinestones, red cabochon eyes, and enameled trim, very likely an unsigned Kenneth Jay Lane piece, 3" tall, *$300.00 – 400.00.* Dragon with faux ivory body and turquoise head, trimmed with diamante rhinestones, signed "KENNETH LANE" with no copyright symbol, 2" x 2", *$400.00 – 500.00.* *Bottom row, left to right:* Trifari seahorse with pearl and enameled accents, signed "Crown Trifari©" on a raised rectangle, 3" tall, *$300.00 – 400.00.* King Neptune, faux jade, coral, and turquoise inserts, attributed to Hattie Carnegie, made in two pieces, unsigned, 2¼" x 2¼", *$500.00 – 600.00.*

Cover design by Terri Hunter
Book design by Lisa Henderson

Collector Books
P.O. Box 3009
Paducah, Kentucky 42002-3009

www.collectorbooks.com

Copyright © 2011 Jacqueline Rehmann

The current values in this book should be used only as a guide. They are not intended to set prices, which vary from one section of the country to another. Auction prices as well as dealer prices vary greatly and are affected by condition as well as demand. Neither the author nor the publisher assumes responsibility for any losses that might be incurred as a result of consulting this guide.

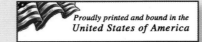
Proudly printed and bound in the
United States of America

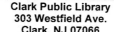

Contents

Dedication

This book is dedicated to Lucille Tempesta. Lucille was the driving force behind the Vintage Fashion and Costume Jewelry collector's club as well as editor of the club's journal. Before her retirement this year, Lucille led the VFCJ for 18 years, through nine conventions, and a membership that included some 8,000 members. Over the years, she dedicated thousands of hours of her own time to bring together vintage costume jewelry collectors from around the world and to present accurate and up-to-date histories of costume jewelry companies and designers. We are all indebted to Lucille for her encouragement, diligence, and hard work.

Acknowledgments

I would like to thank friends who allowed us to photograph their jewelry for this book, including Marianna Schweitzer (Sweetie's Memorable Gemz, Ruby Lane) and Liza Williams (Liza Williams Jewelry, Ruby Lane). My husband and I spent a pleasant spring day at the Schweitzers' home photographing jewelry and enjoying a delicious lunch. I have never met Liza, but that didn't stop her from shipping her plastic jewelry collection to me, no questions asked!

I am grateful to Pat Seal for her help in answering my many questions. Thank you, Pat, for your wonderful friendship.

I wish to thank my sister, whose patient and thorough research ensures the accuracy of information found here.

Several pieces of her jewelry were also photographed for this book.

I thank my mother, whose proofreading skills are unsurpassed. She is also my steadfast and patient shopping buddy! Many of the Christmas tree brooches belong to her.

My husband once again served as photographer. Without his assistance, this project would not have been accomplished. He spent hours designing and building new lights for *Volume 2;* and then spent many more hours photographing jewelry.

My children are able assistants in the hunt for new treasures and many of those treasures are featured in this volume. They are both collectors (of stamps, belt buckles, or jewelry), so they willingly accompany me on shopping expeditions.

Author, Jacqueline Rehmann.

4

Recent Updates in the Field of Costume Jewelry

HAR Mystery Solved

Collectors of vintage costume jewelry have long been captivated by jewelry marked "HAR©." I am one of them. HAR is probably best known for fantastic figural jewelry including beautifully detailed Asian figures with imitation ivory faces, exotic genies, cobras, dragons, and blackamoors. Enameled fruits, small whimsical animals, and more traditional jewelry designs with imitation pearls, rhinestones, faux turquoise, and coral were also made by HAR. Some of the designs include large misshapen stones with an iridescent glow, for which HAR is known. For years, jewelry sleuths have searched for clues about who made the highly desirable designs of HAR. To the delight of collectors everywhere, the mystery was solved when renowned costume jewelry historian Roberto Brunialti and author Susan Klein discovered that the HAR mark was owned by Hargo Creations in New York City. Joseph Heibronner and Edith Levitt founded the company in 1955 shortly after they were married. What's more, some of the most sought after designs, including the dragon and genie pieces, can be dated to April 1959 based on U.S. copyright records. Collectors also learned that the company was short-lived; Heibronner died in August of 1968, which is probably why no records on HAR were found after 1967[1].

Colibri Shuts Its Doors

The Colibri Group unexpectedly shut down on January 20, 2009. Some 280 employees lost their jobs, the majority of whom worked in Providence, Rhode Island. More familiar names known to costume jewelry collectors that were part of the Colibri group are Van Dell and Krementz (see Figure 1 and Figure 2). Van Dell was acquired in 1991 and Krementz was sold to Colibri in 1997. Other than costume jewelry, the company also made watches, clocks, and platinum jewelry and cufflinks. Unfortunately, the company succumbed to current economic conditions.

Figure 1. Krementz ad showing selected items from their 1959 Christmas line.

Price Guide

Values are determined by a combination of factors including condition, design of the piece, rarity, current selling prices, and other price guides. Additional factors such as the

[1] See http://www.illusionjewels.com/Har_Hargo_jewelry.html

location where the item is being sold also affect the selling price. That is the reason for showing a range of values.

There are variations in costume jewelry prices that result from the general state of the economy as well as collector preferences. At times select pieces are "hot" and fetch high prices; as trends change, the value of those pieces will level off while prices for others climb. Jewelry made by DeLizza and Elster, also known as Juliana, is extremely popular as of this book's writing. Prices for a full parure can be several hundred dollars, and rare sets bring even more.

The aspects outlined above help determine the value of costume jewelry and many factors which are key to assigning values tend to remain fairly constant despite fluctuations in economic conditions.

Figure 2: Krementz ad from 1968 showing some of their popular and classic designs.

Introduction

The desire to adorn oneself is basic and enduring, a fundamental aspect of the human psyche. Impervious to hardship and war, it seems rather that such disastrous diversions only inflame human ingenuity. Why else would a prison inmate fiddle with his toothbrush to make a ring, a high school girl make a necklace from colored macaroni, or an American POW use scraps of metal to make a bracelet for his wife?

In the 1930s the memory of the stock market crash lay heavily upon the nation. The decade ended on an equally somber note as the war in Europe unfolded and the U.S. debated its role and then entered the war. Nevertheless the 1930s and 1940s produced some of the most novel, beautifully constructed, and whimsical costume jewelry ever seen. Whether inspired by Hollywood's glamour and the escape it offered, or the pragmatic

and patriotic impulses of a nation at war, costume jewelry was purchased and worn by women across the country.

In the 1930s costume jewelry sales were enormous, despite the economic situation that beset much of the nation. The 'latest' costume jewelry styles featured clips in all sizes and for all occasions. Many were hand-carved using precious woods. Rare woods from every corner of the earth were also cut into initial pins and fobs, bracelets, belt buckles, and buttons. Purple heart, a wood with a lavender cast, clear yellow satinwood from the jungles of Brazil, and ebony and zebrawood from Africa were featured. Jewelry was designed to reveal the wood's natural colorings rather than being camouflaged by paint. Novelty jewelry was popular in the 1930s and was influenced in part by Elsa Schiaparelli and the Surrealist art movement, which greatly affected Ms. Schiaparelli's designs.

Figure 3: In the early 1940s, Mrs. Bundy wasn't using her gas-eating car to shop for groceries.

Figure 4: Carpooling is the "patriotic gesture" in 1942, as this ad states. "Riding around with empty seats is a peacetime luxury."

Figure 5: This is a preview of a recruiting poster that was designed by McClelland Barclay and featured in the January, 1942 issue of *FLYING and Popular Aviation* magazine. McClelland Barclay was an artist who designed costume jewelry which was manufactured by Rice-Weiner. His retro designs are beautifully made and extremely collectible.

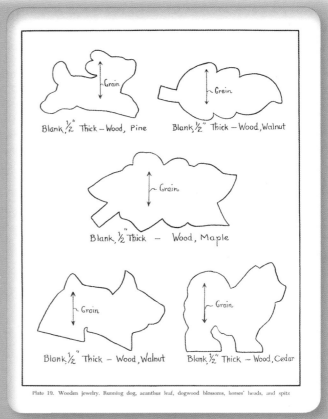

Figure 6: Instructions and patterns for making wooden jewelry. Pets were always a popular theme.

Figure 7: Walco beadcraft insert shows the variety of kits that were available to consumers in 1944.

as well and featured everything from schoolroom charms to household products. In times of economic uncertainty and with precious little to smile about, costume jewelry of the 1930s was good for a chuckle.

The prison arts and crafts movement was another phenomena of the 1930s. In a landmark exhibit, artwork and crafts from inmates at Sing Sing, Clinton Prison, Rhode Island State Prison, Michigan State Prison, the Pennsylvania Industrial School at Hunting, Pennsylvania, and the Reformatory for Women at Framingham, Massachusetts were exhibited at the Sargent Gallery in New York. Mrs. Franklin D. Roosevelt was one of several famous exhibit patrons. Three thousand miles away, Clinton Duffy, warden at San Quentin, was busy putting in place reforms that many called "Clinton's Folly." Duffy's reforms included providing toothbrushes for convicts from which they fashioned rings.

Figure 8: Characteristic fashion accessories of the 1940s included large brooches and fashionable hats.

Insects and animals made from wood and plastic were featured along with more traditional designs using pot metal and rhinestones. Cowboy and Indian brooches and fruit necklaces were popular; three-dimensional outhouses and bucking broncos were worn on ladies' lapels. If women couldn't afford to buy jewelry, they could make it using one of the many kits available; or they could use household items like scraps of fabric and nuts to make jewelry.

Plastic jewelry came onto the costume jewelry scene in a big way too. Massive and colorful, jewelry was carved or made using the modern injection molding techniques of the early 1930s. Thus modern technology helped assure plastic's place in costume jewelry history. In 1937, Lucite was patented by Du Pont. This material would be used by Trifari, Coro, and other companies a few years later to create the fabulous and collectible Lucite jewels that today are more commonly known as 'jelly belly' jewelry.

Gadget jewelry and quirky charm bracelets were popular

Fine Woolens by Hockanum: A tradition of quality in the uniforms of America's Armed Forces since 1809...an unfailing standard of excellence as well in Civilian Life. You will find these woolens today in Clothes planned for your numerous Wartime Activities.

HOCKANUM Woolens

Hockanum Mills, Rockville, Conn. • Founded 1809 • Division of M. T. Stevens & Sons Co., No. Andover, Mass. • J. P. Stevens & Co., Inc., Empire State Bldg., New York, Selling Agents

Figure 9: The military influence was seen in women's fashions in the often subdued colors and slim cut of clothing. Even the depth of hems was dictated by the War Protection Board. "Clothes planned for your numerous Wartime Activities" is how these fashions were advertised.

Mr. Duffy described one inmate in particular who revealed a penchant for making jewelry, a diversion he discovered during solitary confinement. In World War II, the inmate, whose name was Bill, worked tirelessly without pay to fill orders for servicemen who wanted his jewelry for trading in the South Pacific. Bill was so successful that when he left prison, he started a plastics business. After his release he also taught his art to wounded soldiers in army hospitals in his spare time.

In the 1940s, several factors affected the availability of materials that could be used to make costume jewelry. As the United States entered World War II, Americans responded with patriotism and pride. Precious resources that would be needed in the war effort, including rubber, gasoline, and nylon, were conserved across the country. Ads showing workers carpooling or walking became popular. An individual's patriotism was measured by the extent of one's "make do" attitude (see Figures 3 – 5). Brooches made with carved wood were favorites, alone or in combination with other materials. Would-be hobbyists could easily find instructions for carving jewelry designs from wood. Home kits for making wood crafts and jewelry were also popular in the 1940s (see Figures 6 and 7).

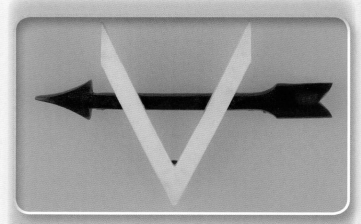

Figure 11: V is for Victory in this simple plastic pin from the early 1940s. Plastic and wood were popular materials due to war shortages. $50.00 – 75.00.

Figure 12: "Thought you would like to carry Harry with you!!" reads the inscription on the original card. This "Buddies" brooch would have been given to a departing soldier as a playful reminder of a loved one. $100.00 – 200.00.

Figure 10: Joseff of Hollywood 1940 wheat pattern brooch in navy blue was made from Tenite, a thermoplastic manufactured by Tennessee Eastman Co. This piece was made in other colors including ivory and dark pink. It measures 3½" x 2". The company diverted jewelry production to war supplies and for two years was dedicated exclusively to the production of precision airplane components for the government. Stamped JOSEFF HOLLYWOOD. $300.00 – 400.00.

Figure 13: Left: Lucite heart worn by a loved one back home. $75.00 – 125.00. Right: marked "CORO Sterling," a "Sweetheart in Service" lapel pin. $50.00 – 75.00.

Women's magazines regularly featured articles that provided instructions for making jewelry from everyday materials including bits of fabric, nuts, macaroni, and pipe cleaners.

Women's clothing styles were determined in part by government orders; even the depth of hems on skirts and dresses was dictated by War Protection Board orders. To conserve fabric, suits were shown with broad shoulders on an otherwise slim silhouette. These classic and conservative designs were ideal for large brooches that were worn by working women. Brooches featuring pearls, glass stones, and loops of metal ribbon were popular (see Figures 8 and 9).

Fashion advertisements encouraged American women to "please the men." An ad in *Vogue* magazine by Eisenberg & Sons, typical of the time period, stated "Women of America, it's your job to look your best, dress appropriately, be gay, cheerful, and active. Buy clothes for conservation, and purchase defense bonds and stamps."

The government also put a limit on ammonia and other chemicals that were used for plating costume jewelry. Early in 1942 Leo Glass & Co. announced that it was going out of business "for the duration." Mr. Glass stated, "we are retiring because we cannot get any of the types of metals which we are accustomed to sell, including brass and white metal, which form the foundation of our business." Mr. Glass further stated that he believed "it was patriotic not even to attempt to manufacture novelties and costume jewelry of raw materials which are essential to the manufacture of defense products."[2] Many companies turned their factories toward wartime production of goods and made items such as caps for bullets and tips for bombshells. Joseff of Hollywood diverted jewelry production to war supplies and for two years the company was dedicated exclusively to the production of precision airplane components for the government. Even after resuming jewelry production, the Joseff

Figure 15: This popular design was rendered most frequently in Bakelite. Here is a wood version which measures 2¼" x 2½". $35.00 – 50.00.

components business continued. Coro operated partially as a prime contractor to the U.S. government and manufactured insignia, parts for bomb nose fuses, and base detonator fuses. Labor shortages also plagued costume jewelry manufacturers. Many employees left jewelry production for defense work which they considered to be more steady.

While many costume jewelry plants famously turned their attention to the production of war related materials, the Colt Patent Firearms Manufacturing Company did something different. They developed a synthetic composition for the manufacture of costume jewelry and in the early 1940s began production of colored stones on a large scale. They noted that "despite the present heavy manufacture of firearms there would soon be room in the present Colt plant to house the new division.[3]

Women made the most of what they had and fashion magazines regularly featured articles showing women how to make their limited wardrobes do double duty. Readers were shown how to transform a daytime suit into an evening ensemble with the addition of a ruffled blouse, a fancy hat, or a piece of costume jewelry.

Figure 14: For the mother with a son in the Army Air Corps, a small lapel pin made from plastic. $25.00 – 40.00.

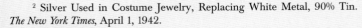

[2] Silver Used in Costume Jewelry, Replacing White Metal, 90% Tin. *The New York Times*, April 1, 1942.

[3] Colt Plant to Make Synthetic Jewelry: It will Produce Costume 'Stones' Formerly Sent by Czechs. *New York Times*, September 17, 1939.

Perhaps it was the idea that it might be the last for a long time, but costume jewelry was selling better than ever. Logically it might seem that everyone would buy just what they needed and items of practical value only. But that was not the case. In addition to costume jewelry consumers were spending money on other items that would boost their morale. Women's hats, in all shapes and sizes, transformed outfits and camouflaged wartime worry and responsibility by adding a festive touch to outfits. Hats were featured in ladies' fashion magazines and Sears catalogs.

White metal, one of the most vital basic metals for the costume jewelry industry, was diverted to the production of war goods while depleted supplies of rhinestones forced manufacturers to talk of closing their doors due to war rationing. The cost of rhinestones jumped from 8 cents to 45 – 55 cents per gross, depending on the size of the stones. Many sizes were unavailable and their use in costume jewelry manufacturing all but ceased. Orders at the prewar prices were no longer being taken because there was no guarantee they could be honored. The less expensive costume jewelry market had a much brighter outlook and several manufacturers shifted their production to jewelry made with wood, glass, plastics, and silver.

Manufacturers of rhinestone jewelry continued to experience shortages even after the war ended. For a few years, it remained difficult to obtain good quality stones at reasonable prices. Jewelry company executives, including Louis Kramer, president of the Kramer Jewelry company, publicly lamented the lack of supplies. In 1947, the best rhinestones were from Austria but the cost of a square cut or shaped stone remained high, costing as much as 60 cents per gross. Other, larger sizes could cost as much as $10.00 per gross. As for the use of metals in jewelry, Gerald Rosenberger, president of Coro, reported that the company would continue to make jewelry from sterling silver regardless of the availability of other metals. He noted that brooches made with sterling were popular and their production would continue as long as they were selling.

Patriotic, western, and South American themes were among the most popular jewelry designs in the early 1940s. These themes were reflected throughout popular culture including movies and advertising. Sweetheart jewelry, sentimental reminders of an absent son or sweetheart, was worn by mothers, wives, and girlfriends awaiting the return of their beloved.

A large, carved heart made of Bakelite was suspended on a key made of the same material. One of the most popular designs of the early 1940s, it was featured on the cover of *Life* magazine in 1941. Many variations of the heart and key motif would be seen throughout the early part of the decade, including ones made of wood or ceramic. A new place to wear this type of brooch was the sleeve. It was shown pinned high on the sleeve of a tailored jacket, giving the effect of a trim emblem.

During WWII, costume or "junk" jewelry played an unlikely role in the Pacific theatre. "Trinket Campaigns" were conducted across the U.S. in which costume jewelry was collected for American soldiers for use in trading with the inhabitants of the Pacific Islands. In their correspondence, soldiers indicated that "natives would bring in wounded, carry supplies and munitions, and perform other difficult tasks for the baubles when money could not induce them to work."[4] In one campaign alone, some 7,000 pieces of jewelry were collected and sent to Colonel Harold G. Hoffman of the Port of Embarkation, who forwarded the jewelry to the troops. One woman brought in a clip in response to a campaign undertaken by the

[4] "Junk Jewelry Sought," *New York Times*, May 25, 1943.

Takahashi

After the bombing of Pearl Harbor, the U.S. government issued an order to relocate Japanese Americans into internment camps. They were given only a few days notice to sell or store their belongings before they were relocated into gated and guarded compounds. Among the Americans sent to the camps were Yoneguma and Kiyoka Takahashi and their three young sons, Joe, Tom, and Jim. The Takahaski family was sent to Poston Camp in Arizona where they remained for three and a half years. Yoneguma and Kiyoka participated in a craft class where they learned how to carve and paint small birds which were made into exquisite brooches. The materials used to create the birds were wooden egg crates, bits of wire clipped from window screens, and twigs found scattered on the ground of the camp. When the family was released, no one would hire Mr. Takahashi. So the couple continued to carve birds as they turned what they learned into a family business that spanned over 40 years. The demand for their lovely birds always exceeded what they could supply. Granddaughter Carol Takahashi remembers how hard her grandparents worked to realize their American dream and said that her grandmother often painted at night and into the early morning hours. In 1988, President Ronald Reagan signed Public Law 100-3, which ensured that people who had been sent to the camps received restitution and an apology from the U.S. government. Just before he died at the age of 95, Mr. Takahashi saw the website that was created by his granddaughter, Carol, to honor the memory of her grandparents and their life's work.

Takahashi birds are unique, colorful, and expertly made. Designs include parrots, pheasants, parakeets, quail, robins, cardinals, owls, and hummingbirds, among others. Matching earrings were made to order but not made after about 1957. The most important clue for collectors is that Takahashi birds never had the screw-in nails to attach pin backs; only push-in nails were used. Only the best bird pieces were signed (with the initials K.T. and perhaps the date). For more information visit the website:

www.takahashibirds.com

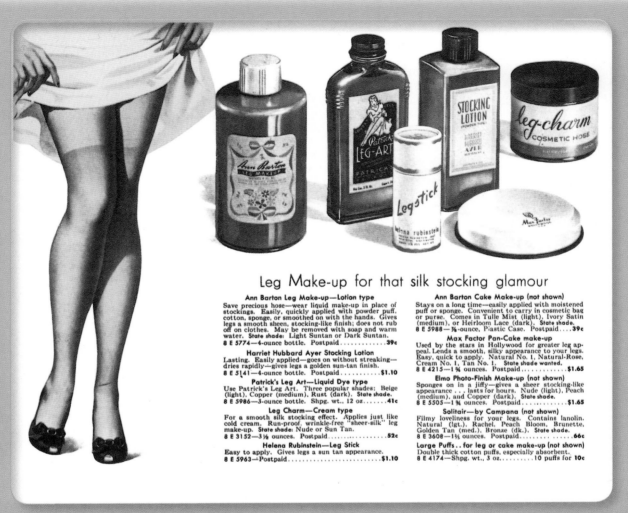

Figure 16: Leg Make-up advertisement from the Sears Catalog, 1942. Photo courtesy of Dover Publications.

Twelfth Night Club at 21 West 47th St. in New York City. She said her daughter always wore the clip on Sunday dates with her boyfriend. "They're engaged now. He's serving somewhere in the South Seas. My daughter asked me to give this clip to your drive."[5]

As manufacturers expanded their lines to counteract the shortage of traditional materials, they experimented successfully with anything but the white or gold-plated metals of other fashion seasons. "Everything from spaghetti to cloth dipped in wax is used for beautiful or amusing gadgets to add an individual touch to the simplest of suits and dresses," proclaimed a *New York Times* article from 1943.[6] Spaghetti, dried and dyed, was treated so it would not get doughy. It was made into necklaces of ten or twelve strands, in monotones and colors, twisted and knotted like ropes. Women were also encouraged to use seashells from former beach excursions. The shells could be tinted and dressed up with pearls or coral pieces. Coro featured jewelry using Caribbean shells which looked like they were painted but whose natural colors only made them appear that way. Wooden jewelry beads were popular too, in some cases embellished with five to six coats of enameled paint. American-made pearls made a substantial contribution to costume jewelry designs in the early 1940s.

Jewelry was made by servicemen at USO clubs. Tiny shells were set on plastic pins and earrings while sawdust

[5] See also Patterson, Dick. *Memories of World War II.* Historical News, Adams County Historical Society, Hastings, NE, Vol. 28, No. 4, 1995.

[6] Simple War Styles Bring Increased Demand for Costume Jewelry: New Materials Used, *New York Times*, February 8, 1943.

Figure 17: As postwar restrictions eased, styles incorporated more fabric and color.

jewelry became popular, which was made by mixing sawdust and glue together. In California, servicemen carved and polished avocado seeds into buttons and brooches or strung them for bracelets. These activities provided relaxation and rehabilitation for veterans and were a source of gifts for family and friends.

Also in California, Elliot Handler began making jewelry as part of a company named Elzac of Hollywood. Handler was designing whimsical and unique figural costume jewelry brooches (See Elzac section).

During the years of World War II, synthetic materials gained wide application and annual production tripled between 1940 and 1945. Two days after the bombing of Pearl Harbor, the Office of Production Management banned sales of rubber tires and tubes to civilians, with the exception of doctors and operators of essential commercial vehicles. Of all the materials needed for the war effort, rubber posed the greatest concern. No less than the success of the Allied effort depended upon the production of synthetic rubber. After a slow start the effort took off and resulted in unparalleled cooperation among academic and corporate laboratories,

university professors, industrial chemists, and chemical companies that had heretofore been fierce competitors.

By 1945 some 1,500 synthetic plastics were available. Plastics were used to make cockpit covers, mortar fuses, and helmet liners among many other things. Nylon was patented in 1937 and went into production by 1938. Of its many uses, nylon stockings were fabulously popular. In May of 1940 the first nylons went on sale in the U.S. They sold out almost immediately – four million pairs in just four days. The euphoria was short-lived as war rationing put an end to the availability of many goods including sugar, coffee, and other items. Of course neither nylon nor silk stockings were available so fashion-conscious working women turned to leg makeup "for the silk stocking glamour" (see Figure 16).

Plastics were used for fountain pens, bathroom fixtures, eyeglasses frames, piano keys, buttons, binoculars, cameras, and costume jewelry. Companies were experimenting with a silvered plastic as a setting. In 1941, plastic jewelry had one of its best seasons ever. Colored Lucite was used to create the effect

Figure 18: Popular mid-century bracelets were made with colorful plastic cabochons in all shapes and sizes. This ad notes the jewelry is by Silver Craft.

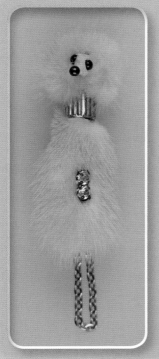

Figure 19: Poodle pin made with real mink has a leather face, gilt collar and chain, and rhinestone trim. Brooch measures 3" tall. $35.00 – 50.00.

Caring for Costume Jewelry: Do's and Don'ts

Since the 1940s women have been told how to care for their costume jewelry. The list includes avoiding direct sunlight, temperature extremes, and moisture, since all can be damaging to costume jewelry. Other tips include treating pin backs, clasps, and other fittings with care; cleaning jewelry regularly, especially when you first acquire it (copper is the exception). Use a non-acidic and nonabrasive cleaner that does not contain ammonia or alcohol. Accumulations of soil can often be found on jewelry where it touched the skin, especially earring backs and the undersides of bracelets. Clean any residue as soon as possible after you purchase jewelry. If left unattended, accumulated residue can lead to verdigris. Plastic jewelry can crack or chip if not handled carefully. Enameled surfaces on jewelry can chip or crack if dropped. Don't polish copper jewelry; a chemical cleaner could strip off the varnish, leaving the copper to rust and corrode. This cannot be stopped once it starts. Celluloid can deteriorate as the result of a "virus." If you have a piece that looks like it is deteriorating, keep it separate from other jewelry because the virus is contagious. A 1960 column in the *New York Times* suggested that to make your rhinestone jewelry look a little less flashy, you should "rub a little cigarette ash and water on them for a quick darkening process." That is a definite "don't!"

Regular cleanings, careful handling, and dry, roomy storage will keep your costume jewelry safe and free from damage. If you need professional assistance for repair and stone replacement, I recommend:
www.MRStones.com

of rhinestones and was used for pins, necklaces, rings, earrings, and bracelets. Indeed, the possibilities seemed limitless.

For the 1943 spring season, the *New York Times* reported that plastic jewelry had emerged from the sporty category and made its way into more dressy ensembles. Coro featured an earrings, bracelet, and necklace ensemble with gigantic plastic calla lilies. A pearlized plastic bowknot and leaf pin with matching earrings set with rhinestones was also featured on the fashion pages of the *New York Times.*

For the most part, interest in improvised adornments made from carved wood and dyed macaroni or seashells faded once the war was over. Fashion magazines proclaimed that when Johnny came marching home again he'd want no reminder of uniforms, dark colors, or a womanless world. With the end of the war, women turned away from every restriction that had been required and sought clothes that were colorful and individualistic. At the same time, they learned during the war the comfort of garments designed for work and did not abandon completely the idea of functional clothing designs like comfortable slacks.

Women's suits began to feature voluminous full skirts with beautifully tailored jackets (see Figure 17). Women had more choices in both fabric and color. The use of synthetic materials for fashions were popular because they were as durable as denim and delicate as fine lace. The postwar evening dress was alluring and colorful, and made more so with the addition of sparkling rhinestone bib necklaces and

chandelier earrings. The horseracing vogue created a market for equine designs. Meanwhile in 1947 Coro launched a line of jewelry that coincided with the opening of Carnegie Hall. Sterling silver brooches in the shape of "violins and brasses" were popular, although expensive.[7]

The 1950s ushered in a new era in the U.S. The postwar baby boom was in full swing and many families acquired televisions sets. The influence of television was to the 1950s what movies were to the 1930s. Fashions featured skirts with poodle appliqués as well as shirtwaist dresses. Costume jewelry was being mass produced, a by-product of streamlined production methods that were perfected during the war. Jewelry companies were selling their jewelry in elaborate boxed sets, often satin lined and elegantly presented. For daytime wear, conservative, tailored costume jewelry was fashionable and featured pearls, circle pins, and single gold hoop bracelets. The pages of fashion magazines presented pearls in all shapes and sizes, from a single demure strand to massive baubles encircling the throat or a Chanel pearl and

[7] "Merchants of Glitter," 5/31/1947, by Elsie McCormick.

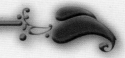

gold chain sautoir (this popular look which included piling on long strands of pearls would emerge again in the 1980s). The color white became popular as revealed in the couture collections of Balenciaga and Dior, who were once again influencing American fashions. Adjustable necklaces rather than fixed-length pieces become very popular and remained so into the 1960s.

Charm bracelets were popular, too. Individual charms to commemorate special occasions such as graduation, vacation travel, or an important birthday were collected and added to bracelets. Costume jewelry charm bracelets also came ready to wear and often featured religious themes such as Coro's Ten Commandment charm bracelet, or Asian faces with sublime Buddhas. Bracelets were made with large, chunky plastic cabochons and squares in vibrant colors (see Figure 18). Some featured the addition of glitter and seashells. Flowers and crowns were popular motifs following the coronation of Queen Elizabeth II. Poodle pins with mink accents were also popular (see Figure 19). Snowflake patterns dripping with rhinestones or brooches that looked like exploding fireworks were featured by companies such as Trifari, Weiss, Eisenberg, Schreiner, and Boucher. The introduction of aurora borealis rhinestones, made possible when Swarovski perfected the finish, was one of the defining moments of the decade for costume jewelry.

In the 1960s plastic beads were extremely popular and they often imitated crystal. Faux pearls and crystal beads were used together with plastic beads to create interesting effects. The medieval style was another popular trend of the 1960s and featured jewelry in all sizes. Maltese cross designs were common and very popular. The Eastern look, made with beads that resembled turquoise, coral, and lapis, were part of the costume jewelry scene of the 1960s. The Asian look was also very fashionable, with plastics being used to imitate ivory and jade. Intense colors were made possible with the use of plastic cabochons. Often jewelry was so large it had to be made of lightweight materials including wood, hollow metal, and plastic pearls. The clothing and jewelry collections of French designer Paco Rabanne caused a sensation in the mid-1960s. His use of wood, leather, aluminum, paper, PVC, and other plastics underscored his belief that "the only new frontier left in fashion is the finding of new materials." The use of avant-garde materials was nothing new for the costume jewelry designs of Schiaparelli, who continued to incorporate plastic, porcelain, and aluminum in her extraordinary designs. Other jewelry designers made their mark in the 1960s including Coppola é Toppo, whose large and extravagant crystal bibs and bracelets were, and remain, enor-

mously popular. In 1962 Kenneth Lane began designing his own collections of jewelry. Of his early jewelry, Mr. Lane said, "I didn't know what was commercial or what had already been done. I just did what I liked..."[8] History would prove that his sense of design and selection of materials were flawless. Butler and Wilson started their business in the late 1960s by selling antique jewelry in London. The jewelry sold very well but supplies were scarce so they started making copies of the jewelry they sold. By the 1980s their bold and beautiful designs were being sold worldwide.

Ethnic styles and natural materials worn by hippies and flower children were available to everyone. The rejection of conventional lifestyles by the 1960s youth movement was reflected in more mainstream jewelry designs. Many companies featured huge flower brooches made from metal and plastic and beaded necklaces made with wood, cork, stone, and plastic beads. By the early 1970s the "back to nature" influence was in full swing. Jewelry was also influenced by southwest American Indian designs and Egyptian motifs revealed in the enormously popular King Tut exhibit which garnered long lines in every city it visited. Larry Vrba's designs for Miriam Haskell included the popular Egyptian line. He also designed, for Castlecliff, one of their most popular lines, a series of large and colorful Indian-inspired pendants and pins.

In the early 1970s, Carolee also began selling costume jewelry, and is most noted for her copies of the Duchess of Windsor jewels; the copies were instant hits. In 1975 Butler and Wilson designed one of their most collectible series, including Pierrot bracelets, brooches, and necklaces which were etched and painted Galalith.

As the decade wore on, working women were dressing for success. The formula included conservative suits in subdued colors and styles, accented with understated accessories that were not overly feminine. Appropriate, conservative attire would help ensure that women be taken seriously in a traditionally male, white collar world. Meanwhile, for many costume jewelry companies, sales plummeted. It was during the 1970s that many closed their doors including Beau Jewels, Boucher, Capri, Carl-Art, Hattie Carnegie, Castlecliff, Goldette, Hollycraft, and Coro.

In the 1980s costume jewelry designs were once again glamorous, witty, and exciting. By the middle of the decade, when television stars were setting the standard with their beautiful pearls and rhinestones, the costume jewelry industry was earning well over $2 billion a year.

The following vintage advertisements illustrate the evolution of costume jewelry style through the decades.

[8] See Lane, Kenneth Jay. *Faking it*. Harry N. Abrams, Inc., New York, NY, 1996.

Figure 20: **Adele Simpson ad from March 1950. Adele Simpson was a fashion designer who made costume jewelry to complement her fashions.**

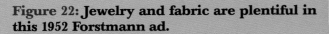

Figure 21: **September 1951 ad featuring fashions by Adele Simpson. Note the coordinating rhinestone jewelry.**

Figure 22: **Jewelry and fabric are plentiful in this 1952 Forstmann ad.**

Figure 23: Coro jewelry is featured in this ad from 1955. Matching sets with adjustable necklaces were popular and featured rhinestone and gold-tone designs.

Figure 24: Coro jewelry is featured in this ad from 1957. Matching sets and adjustable necklaces were popular and featured a variety of pearls, plastic, and gold-tone designs.

Figure 25: Lovely ad from 1955 features yards of synthetic fabric (Chromspun acetate fiber by Eastman), fabulous rhinestone jewelry, and rhinestone-accented buttons.

Figure 26: **The perfect jewelry box to hold costume jewelry of the 1950s, "whether her jewels be precious as a rajah's ransom or casual as cocktails for two..."**

Figure 27: **In the 1950s working women wore classic designs featuring understated pearls.**

Figure 28: **In this ad from April 1955, Kramer features a line of porcelain jewelry encircled with rhinestones called Bon Bon. "Delicious mounds of delicate porcelain circled with rhinestones. A jeweler's confection in white, pink, blue, yellow, or jet."**

Figure 29: Lisner ad from 1958 features jewelry with "turquoise-colored stones created by the chemical skill of man."

Figure 30: Gorgeous bead and pearl bracelets by Castlecliff, "the talked-about jewelry."

Figure 31: Krementz ad from 1955. Krementz jewelry was marketed as made "in the tradition of precious jewelry."

Figure 32: Furs and tiaras were popular evening wear in the 1950s, as seen in this ad from November 1958. This coat is made from Verel, "Eastman's new acrylic fiber."

Regina® Glenara and Donnybrook make International Fashion New

gina Glenara by Donnybrook is the coat a smart mink would give his lady love to make a lasting impression! Although Re-

Figure 33: Coro ad from 1958 shows two sets of Coro jewelry including Riviera and Empress. "America's best dressed women wear Coro jewelry."

The switch is to the RIPPLESTITCH

This is the bulky stitch that's the like of which you never saw before. The ripplestitch looks hand-knit with a bit more elegance. The ripplestitch is a Carlisle exclusive, made of terrific Tycora yarn to keep for keeps its buoyant beauty. Shown in a nifty cardigan at $10.95; a spiffy chemise at $12.95. White, black, maize, jockey red, cornflower blue, russet, green. Sizes 34-40. At nice stores, or write Carlisle Sportswear, 1410 Broadway, New York 18.

CARLISLE sweaters of tycora®

Figure 34: Sweater of synthetic fibers ("terrific Tycora") is accented with plastic beaded necklaces in this ad from November 1958.

Figure 35: 1959 ad features beaded necklaces made with plastic and glass crystals by Marvella.

Figure 36: Marvelustre® simulated pearls called Colossa® are featured in this beautiful Marvella ad from September 1960.

Figure 37: Marvella "casts a beautiful spell" in this ad from 1964. Synthetic pearls are called Marvellissimo®, "precisely simulated pearls of synthetic brilliance. Who'd suspect such cunning – from a lovely charmer like you?"

Figure 38: Weiss ad from October 1964 features large, chandelier-style rhinestone earrings and brooches.

Figure 39: Huge rhinestone brooch and bracelet are featured in this fashion spread from the early 1960s.

Figure 40: **Francois ad from the 1960s features a magnificent matching set of necklaces, bracelet, brooch, and earrings. Francois was a division of Coro.**

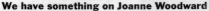

Figure 41: **The beautiful and talented actress Joanne Woodward, wearing large simulated pearls by Richelieu, is featured in this October 1963 ad.**

We have something on Joanne Woodward

Something new. Something stupendous. Our 3-strands of simulated pearls, bathed in a warm new rosé glow, to wear high and proud and beautiful as you see them here on Joanne Woodward, $10. Equally new and stupendous, the spectacular pin, $30. Earrings to match, $25. All plus tax. At the very best stores throughout the U.S. and Canada.

Richelieu

SEE JOANNE WOODWARD AND PAUL NEWMAN STARRING IN "A NEW KIND OF LOVE"

Plastics

ince their discovery, the influence of plastics on every aspect of life has been pervasive and profound. During the Great Depression the plastics industry was one of the few to thrive. The manufacture of costume jewelry was one of the greatest successes of this industry.

At the 1939 World's Fair, the potential of new plastics was on parade. Visitors saw the first use of nylon, modeled by beautiful women who pulled back their flared skirts to reveal long nylon-sheathed legs while others played an endless game of tug-of-war to demonstrate the elasticity of the new material at the Du Pont exhibit.[9] Du Pont's Lucite, the new crystal clear polymethyl methacrylate plastic, was also on display, as was its rival Plexiglas from Rohm and Haas.

At the Du Pont exhibit, plastics were used for shoe bows, lipstick containers, walking sticks, and jewelry including necklaces and bracelets, which were made with new pearl effects. The Rohm & Haas exhibit featured instruments made of Plexiglas including a flute and a violin. Fair souvenirs included celluloid badges and a special Bakelite electric razor made by Remington that was emblazoned with the Fair logo. In the 1940s the use of plastics expanded to include household items such as clothespins, porch furniture, heels for shoes, phonograph record holders, salt and pepper shakers, handles on kitchen utensils, telephones, and kitchen canisters. During an exhibition sponsored by *Modern Plastics* magazine, more than 1,000 entries of plastic items were featured. It was noted that because "the plastic articles are lightweight, non-spottable, colorfast, slow to conduct heat, and easily cleaned, they are an excellent medium for many household objects."

In the 1960s, plastics, more than any other material, symbolized the ideology of "pop" culture. Plastics were used to make all kinds of jewelry, the bigger and brighter the better. The plastics industry during this time was also investing a great deal in developing new polymers. By 1982, plastic production surpassed that of steel worldwide. The Plastic Age had definitely arrived.

Today, plastic costume jewelry is a collectible category all its own. In addition to early pieces fashioned wholly from plastic, almost all costume jewelry designers featured a line of jewelry made with plastic accents. For some companies, Lisner for example, the plastic pieces set in gold tone or silver tone became their most popular. Kenneth Jay Lane's fabulous figural jewelry made liberal use of plastics, including enormous color-saturated cabochons and shimmering pearls, to achieve Mr. Lane's masterful designs. The jewelry of Joseff of Hollywood, Sarah Coventry, Napier, Hattie Carnegie, Miriam Haskell, Monet, Trifari, Nettie Rosenstein, HAR, and many others used plastics to achieve large and lightweight designs that would be comfortable to wear. Sometimes it is difficult to differentiate plastics from stone or glass due to the fantastic range of effects that were achieved. However, both stone and glass are much heavier than plastics and cold to the touch, while plastics are relatively light and warm to the touch.

> "Just as a rag, a bone, and a hank of hair may be used to describe that extraordinary creation known as woman, so carbolic acid, soya beans and sour cow's milk might be used to designate the myriad fantastic, rainbow-hued objects which come under the common designation of plastics."
>
> LIFE *Magazine, 1940*

In its broadest sense, the term "plastic" refers to materials that can be molded or shaped by applying heat or pressure. A more contemporary definition of "plastic" and one that is more useful in understanding the jewelry shown in this book, refers to a synthetic organic compound known as a polymer which can be molded, carved, and pressed into shape. Some synthetic plastics were filled with gold, glitter, or seashells for added interest. Bakelite, the first fully synthetic plastic material, was fashioned from man-made molecules that have no precise duplicate in nature. Now that's synthetic.

My research took me to the mid-nineteenth century when brilliant chemists around the world were experimenting in their laboratories. It soon became apparent that an advanced degree in chemistry would be useful to decode the terminology surrounding this complex topic. Even more startling was that some authors advocated the use of testing methods to determine the type of plastic used that were potentially destructive. In the end, I believe that what most collectors really care about is whether a Bakelite bangle with injected dots (and the big price tag) is authentic or one of the thousands of "Fakelite" pieces in the collectibles market. Testing methods do's and don'ts are shown in Table 1 on the following page.

---

[9] See Fenichell, Stephen. *Plastic: The Making of a Synthetic Century,* for more amusing anecdotes about plastics.

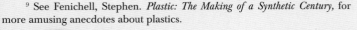

Table 1: Testing Methods: Do's and Don'ts

Some popular reference books advocate the use of the hot pin test to determine the type of plastic used to make an item. This method is harmful and destructive and is a definite "don't."

Many (but not all plastics) used in the production of costume jewelry give off distinct odors when heated, either by rubbing vigorously or running under warm water for 20 – 30 seconds. This smell test is a simple and non-intrusive way to determine the type of plastic used. If the jewelry is trimmed with rhinestones, made with wood, or trimmed with metal, it is not advisable to run the piece under water. The chart below lists selected plastics and the smell they give off when heated.

Material	Odor
Cellulose nitrate	Camphor
Cellulose acetate	Vinegar
Phenol formaldehyde	Acrid phenol (phenol is carbolic acid and is used for synthesizing phenol-formaldehyde; some have likened this smell to a burnt resistor)
Urea formaldehyde	Formaldehyde; earliest versions of urea plastics (thioureas) will have a sulfur smell
Casein	Burned milk

Formula 409™, Simichrome, Scrubbing Bubbles, or Bakelite test solutions can be applied with a cotton swab to the surface of Bakelite jewelry and will show up as a faint to strong yellow stain on the cotton if the piece is Bakelite. The product works by dissolving some of the surface oxidation that is normally present on the jewelry surface. If the piece has been treated then it cannot be successfully tested in this way. The bottom line: these are potentially destructive tests which will damage the finish of your piece.

The fact is that to determine the chemical compound of your plastic jewelry, it is impossible to tell conclusively without damaging or destroying the piece.[10]

A few key references were extremely helpful in sorting through the enormous amount of information on synthetic plastics. These references are presented in Table 2. Vintage advertisements also provide invaluable references and can be most helpful for dating jewelry.

Table 2: Key Plastics References[11]

Author	Title
Baker, Lillian	*Plastic Jewelry of the Twentieth Century* (updated by Karima Parry and Ginger Moro)
DiNoto, Andrea	*Art Plastic: Designed for Living*
Ettinger, Roseann	*20th Century Plastic Jewelry*
Klein, Susan	*Mid-Century Plastic Jewelry*
Lauer, Keith and Julie Robinson	*Celluloid: Collector's Reference and Value Guide*
Moro, Ginger	*European Designer Jewelry*
Parry, Karima	*Bakelite Pins*

[10] Janik, Tracy. "Myth busters – Urban Legends of Black Bakelite," *VFCJ*, Volume 17, No. 3, 2007.

[11] See bibliography for additional information and references.

The Modern Age of Plastics began officially at the 1862 International Exhibition in London, a show that attracted 29,000 exhibitors and six million visitors. It was here that Parkesine, a plastic that could be shaped into combs, decorative boxes, and decorative medallions, made its debut.[12] Parkesine was not especially successful because Parkes used inferior products to cut production costs. His use of castor oil caused problems and the items he made from his plastic Parkesine were highly flammable.

A growing shortage of ivory billiard balls ensured that the work of Parkes would not be in vain. John Wesley Hyatt wanted to win a $10,000 prize that was being offered by the billiards supplier Phelan and Collander to the first person who could made a non-ivory billiard ball. In 1868 Hyatt mixed collodion with camphor, left out the castor oil, and ground the mixture into a powder. When he put the powder into a mold under heat and pressure, it fused into a clear, solid material which he called "celluloid." It proved to be an extremely popular material and useful for making many items despite its flammability. Celluloid could be planed or worked on a lathe when cold, molded or rolled, or extruded when warm. It was used to make eyeglasses frames, piano keys, dolls, jewelry, and decorative hair combs, while pink celluloid replaced rubber in false teeth. Celluloid could be tinted or made black, white, or clear (see Figure 42).

Celluloid's most important contribution was to photography; most of the celluloid produced was used for making photographic film, but its flammability encouraged researchers to search for other materials. In 1900 the French scientist Henri Dreyfuss produced "safety film" by substituting acetic acid (vinegar) for nitric acid in the celluloid formula to make cellulose acetate.

Most vintage plastic jewelry was made from two basic categories of plastics including thermoset and thermoplastic plastics. These terms are often used interchangeably, but there is a clear distinction between them. Thermoset plastics become soft when heated but are heated again to set their shape. After the second heating, they never become soft again (much like a clay pot). Bakelite is a thermoset plastic. Thermoplastics can be heated, molded, and cooled then reheated and remolded. Thermoplastics will always soften and become plastic when heated and harden when cool. Thermoplastics keep their shape until they are heated again. Celluloid is in this category. Additional plastics, as well as selected popular trade names, are shown in Table 3.

Celluloid and Bakelite are trade names but it has become common practice for these trade names to be used to describe all pyroxylin and phenol-formaldehyde plastics. In the same way Galalith is used to describe casein products.

Table 3: Plastics Used to Make Costume Jewelry

Thermoset	Thermoplastic
1904 – Caseins (Galalith, Erinoid, Ameroid)	1868 – Pyroxylin or cellulose nitrate[13] (Celluloid, pyralin, French ivory)
1908 – Phenol-formaldehyde or phenolics-cast and molded (Bakelite, Catalin, Prystal, Marbelette)	1894 – Cellulose acetate (Tenite, Lumarith)
1928 – Urea formaldehyde (Beetleware or Beetle, Plaskon, Duroware, Uralite)	1901 – Acrylics (Plexiglas 1931) and Lucite (1937)
1939 – Epoxy resins	1929 – Polystyrenes (Styrol)

Figure 42: **Antique card advertising "Celluloid waterproof collars, cuffs, & shirt bosoms."**

[12] In 1845 Christian Friedrich Schonbein took cellulose, a plentiful material found in cotton balls, cotton wool, and wood pulp, and dissolved it with a mixture of sulfuric and nitric acids to create cellulose nitrate. He patented it under the name "gun cotton," so called because of its explosive quality. Building on the work of Schonbein, Parkes used collodion ("gun cotton" combined with a mixture of ether and alcohol), added castor oil and camphor, reduced the amount of nitric acid, and added color to make Parkesine.

[13] These are partial lists; in *Celluloid: Collector's Reference and Value Guide* by Keith Lauer and Julie Robinson, some 65 trade names are listed for cellulose nitrate plastics.

When Baekeland's patent for Bakelite expired in 1927, the American Catalin Corporation marketed Catalin, a cast phenolic resin, which was available in a full spectrum of colors (unlike Bakelite). Catalin was also different than Bakelite in that it required no fillers and could be manufactured in mottled, solid, translucent, or even transparent finishes. Today the distinction between Bakelite and Catalin is often blurred and most references describe the family of phenol-formaldehyde plastics simply as Bakelite. See Table 4 for more examples of trade names that have come into common usage.

Table 4: Plastics and Trade Names in Common Usage

Type of Plastic	Trade Names	Trade Name in Common Usage
Phenolic resins	Bakelite, Catalin, Prystal, Marbelette	Bakelite
Caseins	Galalith, Erinoid, Ameroid	Galalith
Urea formaldehyde	Beetleware, Plaskon, Duroware, Uralite	Beetle
Pyroxylin or cellulose nitrate	Celluloid, Pyralin, French Ivory	Celluloid
Acrylics	Plexiglas and Lucite	Lucite

Celluloid Jewelry

Celluloid jewelry and accessories were manufactured at the Celluloid Novelty Company in Newark, New Jersey. The earliest celluloid jewelry reflected traditional Victorian era designs and featured realistic animal designs, mourning brooches, cameos, bracelets, necklaces, pendants, and pins. These were manufactured in imitation coral, ivory, and tortoiseshell. Trade names for celluloid included Ivorine, Fiberlite, Ivory Fiberloid, and Ivory-Grained Celluloid. In 1924, William Lindsey, a chemist at the Celluloid Novelty Company, discovered that when he applied warm mercury to the surface of celluloid, a chemical reaction resulted which created a beautiful pearlescent effect. By the end of the 1920s, pearlescent laminated celluloid became a huge commercial success and was used to make jewelry, buttons, and buckles.

After World War II, the Japanese relied on their celluloid industry to help rebuild their economy. From 1945 to 1952, during the occupation of Allied troops, the Japanese made and exported inexpensive novelty pins and rings. These were frequently embellished with hand painting, which resulted in almost garish colors. Japanese celluloid has a thick, shiny appearance and the items made were often signed.

Celluloid Hair Ornaments and Combs

Leominster, Massachusetts was the center of natural plastics comb manufacturing in the U.S. during the eighteenth and nineteenth centuries. Cattle horn and tortoiseshell were used to make the combs but the process was labor intensive and very time consuming. The Hawks Bill turtle, source of the tortoise shell, was nearing extinction due to its use in hair ornaments and other items.

By the mid-1870s, celluloid became the material of choice for combs and hair ornaments. It was easy to use because it could be manipulated and dyed to imitate luxury materials. Ornaments were often decorated with metal, rhinestones, and paint. The majority of hair combs available today in the collectibles market was produced in the early twentieth century. An American dancer and actress, Irene Castle, bobbed her hair in 1919 and almost overnight half the comb factories in Leominster shut down. During the late 1920s there was a brief revival of interest in the large, Spanish-style back combs that were made to look like tortoiseshell or amber. These were worn by women with both short hair and long hair. But the revival was short-lived. The Depression brought a final end to the era of fancy celluloid hair combs.

Casein

Casein is a semi-synthetic plastic which originates from milk curds that are washed, dried, powdered, and then kneaded with water into a plastic dough. In 1899, Adolf Spitteler discovered that when he added formaldehyde, it reacted with the casein to make it hard and resistant to water and acids. Casein was used to make buttons, buckles, knitting needles, and jewelry.

Bakelite

When Dr. Leo H. Baekeland patented his invention in 1909, no one could have foreseen the hammer prices of certain costume jewelry pieces some 75 or so years later. In fact, the first fully synthetic plastic and the "material of

a thousand uses" was mainly used for utilitarian purposes including handles for irons and pots, switches, radio and television components, and even coffins. George Eastman used Bakelite for end pieces of his Kodak cameras. During World War I, Bakelite was used for electrical insulation and to strengthen brake linings in equipment and vehicles used in the war. Bakelite was used to make costume jewelry, buttons, and buckles from the late 1920s to the mid-1950s. Collectors agree that the most exquisitely crafted Bakelite jewelry was made between the mid-1940s until about 1950.

Butler & Wilson, Kenneth Jay Lane, and Diane Von Furstenberg are contemporary designers who continued to use Bakelite in their designs. In general, however, Bakelite's popularity began to fade as fashions changed in the 1950s. The quality and amount of workmanship required to make a piece of fancy Bakelite jewelry (which now helps determine the value of a piece) is one of the reasons the popularity of this material declined. Heavily carved, highly articulated, and dimensional pieces are desirable; also pierced work, hand painting, lamination, reverse carving, artistic use of non-Bakelite elements as inlays, or other accents all increase the value of a piece.

Tenite

Tenite is a trade name for cellulose acetate. Tenite was made by Tennessee Eastman and is of interest to costume jewelry collectors as the plastic used by Joseff of Hollywood to make some of his jewelry. Tenite was also used to make the first Frisbee, which became an instant sensation and took over where the hula hoop left off. Walter Frederick Morrison designed a flying plastic disk made from Tenite and first called it Li'l Abner, then the Pluto Platter, finally settling on the name Frisbee after tin pie plates.[14]

Plastics Timeline

Key events in the development of plastics are shown in the timeline below. The dates represent when the material was patented and/or presented to the public. Decades of experimentation and discovery often went into the development of plastics; each date should be considered in the context of this long development cycle.

Plastic jewelry is in a category all its own. Celluloid or Bakelite, Lucite or Plexiglas, it is popular, collectible, and certainly habit-forming!

1845 *Christian Friedrich Schoenbine develops cellulose nitrate.*

1862 *Alexander Parkes displays his new invention, Parkesine, at the International Exhibition in London, for which he wins a bronze medal.*

1865 *French chemist Paul Schutzenberger discovers cellulose acetate by combining cellulose with acetic acid (vinegar) instead of nitric acid.*

1868 *John Wesley Hyatt obtains a patent for celluloid and soon establishes the American Celluloid Corporation.*

1897 *Spitteler & Krische discover how to make Casein from skimmed milk.*

1909 *Leo Hendrik Baekeland patents Bakelite, the first synthetic thermosetting plastic.*

1924 *British scientists substitute urea (ammonia & carbon dioxide) for phenol in formaldehyde formula to obtain a thermosetting molding powder with new color range including white.*

1928 *In the U.S., American Cynamid Company introduces a urea-formaldehyde resin ("Beetle") and brightly colored Bakelite-type material becomes available.*

1931 *Acrylic plastics are developed in Germany by Dr. Otto Rohm. His company, Rohm & Haas, introduces Plexiglas® in 1931.*

1937 *Du Pont introduces Lucite® and Dow Chemical brings polystyrene to the U.S. (polystrene was first synthesized by French scientist Marcellin Berthellot in 1869).*

1939 *Swiss chemist Dr. Pierre Castan patents epoxy resins; they are introduced into the marketplace in 1946.*

1982 *Plastic production surpasses that of steel worldwide; the Plastic Age formally begins.*

---

[14] Shortly after the Civil War, William Russell Frisbie opened a bakery in Bridgeport, Connecticut, which became popular with the students from Yale. Frisbie's pie tins were stamped with his name (Frisbie). Evidently when the Yale students were bored, they took to sailing the discarded Frisbie pie tins across campus and sounded an alarm when doing so, yelling "Frisbie!" every time a tin went whizzing by.

Jewelry Patents

Precious and non-precious jewelry designs and mechanisms were protected by design and utility patents. Design patents were used to protect from copying the way a piece of jewelry looked and have a maximum duration of seven years.

Utility patents protect against copying the way an article or mechanism works. Utility patents covered such things as clasps, earring backs, and duette mechanisms.

The numbering system differs for design and utility patents. Design patents are six digit numbers; utility patents have seven.

While design patents may be useful for approximately dating jewelry, this is not always the case. Some companies continued to make popular designs long after their patent protection expired.

Since utility patents cover a much longer period of time, they are less useful for dating items. They are nevertheless an important source of historical information.

The copyright law was amended in 1947 so jewelry companies could copyright their jewelry designs. Even so, companies were slow to avail themselves of the benefits of copyright protections. That was until a successful lawsuit by Trifari against the Charel Jewelry Company brought the matter to the attention of jewelry companies. Thereafter, the use of the copyright symbol (©) became more commonplace and is an integral part of jewelry signatures from the mid-1950s.

Figure 43: 1940s ad from the Bakelite Corporation, a "Unit of Union Carbide and Carbon Corporation." It shows a variety of plastics including injection-molded polystyrene, crystal and pearlescent jewelry from cast resin rods, compression-molded radio cabinets, and transparent shoes made from Vinylite plastic sheeting. It reads, "all plastics are not alike. There are important differences not only in forms and fabrication methods, but also in service and styling characteristics. All of these play an essential part in proper plastics selection."

Celluloid Combs

In 1906, Leominster, Massachusetts featured some 13 comb manufacturers in the city's directory. Hair combs were also manufactured in France, Scotland, and Germany. By the 1920s, the appetite for more variety was revealed with added decorative treatments including rhinestones, pearls, and paint.

Then the unthinkable happened. Women started bobbing their hair. Almost overnight, half of the comb factories in Leominster shut down. The fashion for wearing Spanish-style combs with long, dangling earrings kept the comb business alive for awhile. But by the end of the decade combs were rarely, if ever worn.[15]

[15] For an excellent and comprehensive history of combs, see *The Comb: Its History and Development*, by Jen Cruse, Robert Hale Limited, 2007.

Lovely celluloid chignon comb features pearl and metal accents. It measures 6" long x 3" wide. $50.00 – 75.00.

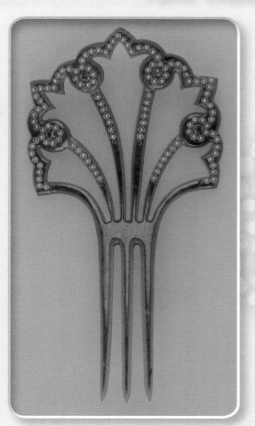

Celluloid backcomb features red rhinestone accents. 5" at widest x 6" long. $75.00 – 100.00.

Pavé-set clear stones are featured with tiny paint accents in this beautiful celluloid backcomb made to look like tortoiseshell. 7" long x 3½" at widest. $75.00 – 100.00.

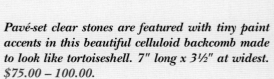

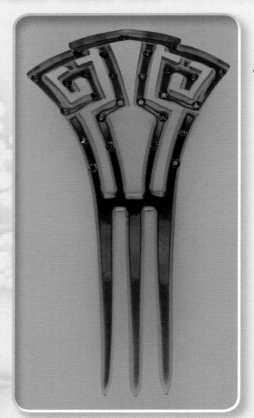

This beautiful chignon comb features blue stones. $35.00 – 50.00.

Chignon comb featuring clear and colored stones. $35.00 – 60.00.

Chignon comb featuring metal trim. $35.00 – 60.00.

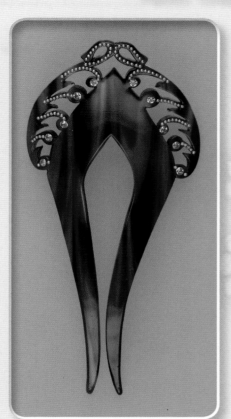

Chignon comb featuring clear stones. $35.00 – 60.00.

Chignon comb featuring clear stones. $35.00 – 60.00.

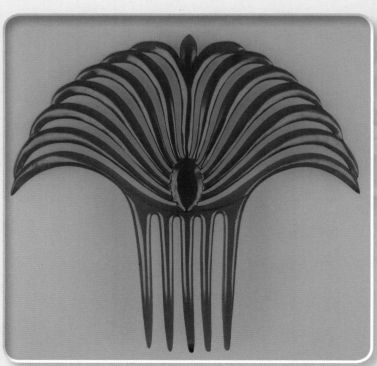

Fabulous Art Deco design backcomb. Measures 7" at widest x 6½" long. $75.00 – 100.00.

Rare signed faux tortoise comb. Measures 5½" x 7½" long. Signature is heat-stamped Auguste Bonaz and is barely decipherable. $150.00 – 200.00.

Fancy backcomb with exotic bird motif. Measures 8½" at widest x 7¾" long. Some of the watermark design has worn away. $75.00 – 100.00.

Evidence of watermark can be seen in this celluloid backcomb with green rhinestone accents. It measures 6" at widest x 5" long. $50.00 – 75.00.

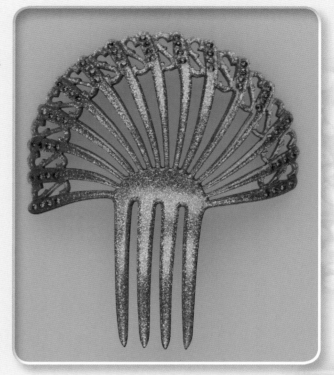

Imitation goldstone backcomb with green rhinestone accents. Measures 4½" tall x 5½" at widest. $75.00 – 100.00.

This amber colored celluloid comb is almost iridescent. It measures 4" at widest x 6" tall. $50.00 – 75.00.

This magnificent faux tortoise comb features an Art Deco design. Measures 8½" tall x 5" at widest. $50.00 – 75.00.

Fabulous Deco design in black celluloid. Measures 4" wide x 8" tall. $50.00 – 75.00.

Rare bandeau features crystal clear rhinestone trim set into faux tortoise celluloid. This delicate piece is completely intact. $300.00 – 400.00 and up.

Celluloid Jewelry

Coral colored celluloid brooch features pink cabochon and faux pearl accents in a metal setting. This brooch measures 3" x 2". $50.00 – 75.00.

Art Deco design is reflected in these two brooches.
Top: Celluloid with pearlescence and rhinestone trim. In 1902, the patent for setting rhinestones in celluloid was issued. In 1925 colored pearlescence was first introduced, so this brooch dates to after that time. It measures 3½" long. $75.00 – 100.00.
Bottom: Deco design in black onyx colored celluloid with rhinestone trim; imitation onyx was perfected in 1893. This brooch also measures 3½" long and has a curve to it. $75.00 – 100.00.

Early celluloid floral brooch features topaz and green rhinestones, paint details; it measures 2¾" tall. $50.00 – 75.00.

Art Deco style celluloid brooch features pavé-set topaz rhinestones; it measures 2" wide x 2½" tall. $50.00 – 75.00.

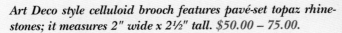

Celluloid parrot on perch features green rhinestone accents. This fellow measures 2¼" tall. $50.00 – 75.00.

Celluloid animals have brass settings; also colorful rhinestone and paint details. The mythological Pegasus (left) measures 2½" wide. $50.00 – 75.00; the demure lamb measures 1½" x 1". $25.00 – 50.00; and the giraffe is 3" tall x 1" wide. $50.00 – 75.00.

Creamy celluloid cameo has a brass setting and measures 2" tall x 1½" wide. A lovely example of an older celluloid cameo. $75.00 – 100.00.

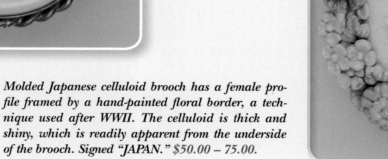

Molded Japanese celluloid brooch has a female profile framed by a hand-painted floral border, a technique used after WWII. The celluloid is thick and shiny, which is readily apparent from the underside of the brooch. Signed "JAPAN." $50.00 – 75.00.

This 1920s pendant measures 2½" long and is suspended on a grosgrain ribbon; the marbled green celluloid is accented with green rhinestones. The opaque green color is unusual. $100.00 – 150.00.

Green marbled celluloid locket on celluloid chain features paint trim. Celluloid chains were made by the Viscoloid company in Leominster, Massachusetts; the plain ovals were hand joined by women who took the material home and assembled them in their spare time. Their payment was based on the finished length of chain.[16] $100.00 – 150.00.

Lovely lightweight celluloid necklace features amber and root beer colored leaves and flowers on a celluloid chain. Note the cluster of flowers in the center of the 15" chain. $100.00 – 150.00.

[16] Lauer, Keith and Julie Robinson. *Celluloid: Collector's Reference and Value Guide.* Collector Books, Paducah, KY, 1999, pg. 63.

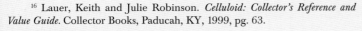

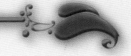

Light as a feather celluloid necklace features delicate pastel colored leaves on a celluloid chain. The chain slips over the simple ring closing. $75.00 – 125.00.

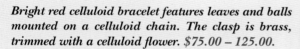

Bright red celluloid bracelet features leaves and balls mounted on a celluloid chain. The clasp is brass, trimmed with a celluloid flower. $75.00 – 125.00.

Classic Art Deco design is featured in this opaque green belt buckle. There are no metal components on this buckle; the loops on the back are celluloid also. When assembled the buckle measures 2½" wide x 2" high. $50.00 – 75.00.

This pretty celluloid belt buckle has clear rhinestone trim and is signed "JAPAN." $35.00 – 50.00.

Heart-shaped celluloid brooch features plenty of detail and measures 1¾" x 1¾". $40.00 – 65.00.

Creamy celluloid is on display in these pieces; a pair of 1930s dress clips are trimmed with clear rhinestones and measure 1¾" x 1¾". $50.00 – 75.00.

A pretty molded fruit bowl features clear rhinestone trim. It measures 2½" wide x 1¾". $50.00 – 75.00.

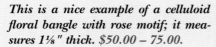

This is a nice example of a celluloid floral bangle with rose motif; it measures 1⅛" thick. $50.00 – 75.00.

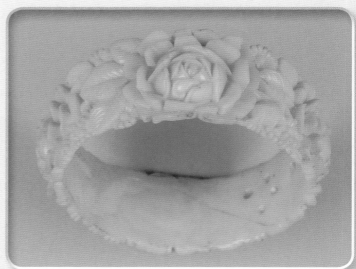

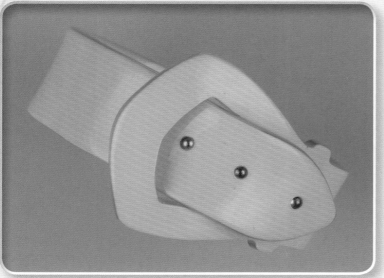

Later cellulose acetate buckle bangle features metal accents. Non-flammable cellulose acetate was first introduced during the 1930s and quickly took over where celluloid left off; it had all the qualities that consumers enjoyed about celluloid, but it was not flammable. $75.00 – 125.00.

Celluloid bangles feature rhinestone trim, painted and carved details. From the left, octagon-shaped thin bangle, $40.00 – 65.00; triple rows of rhinestones are featured in this wider bangle, $125.00 – 175.00; carved and painted bangles, $75.00 – 125.00 each.

Celluloid bracelets with rhinestones were sometimes worn above the elbow. $125.00 – 175.00 each.

Magnificent example of celluloid bracelet, in beautiful condition. $200.00 – 300.00.

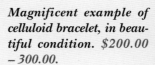

Delicate celluloid bracelet has clasp, fruit trim. $75.00 – 125.00.

Bakelite

It is helpful to know some chief characteristics of Bakelite to aid identification and avoid a disappointing buying experience.

Bakelite is heavier than other types of plastic of the same size including Lucite and celluloid (note: a piece of "Fakelite" can actually be heavier than a similar size piece of Bakelite).

Two pieces of Bakelite that come into contact with one another produce a distinctive "thunk" as opposed to a clink.

Running a piece of Bakelite under hot water should produce a unique formaldehyde-type odor. Rigorously rubbing the surface may also produce the same smell.

Pin backs can be riveted/screwed or heat set; later pieces, for example earrings, can have backs which are glued on (1950s – 1960s). The hardware on a brooch can be a one- or two-piece pin back, and have a simple c- or roll-over clasp.

In general there are a number of factors that affect value including many of the same factors that affect the value of any piece of vintage costume jewelry. These include condition, craftsmanship, design, and rarity. Condition is self explanatory; a crack or chip will greatly affect value unless it is an extremely rare piece. However, this is the exception. Generally pieces that have suffered damage lose value. Repaired findings reduce value as well. The craftsmanship and design of a piece affects value; for example, how intricate is the carving? What specialty decorative techniques were used (specialty decorative techniques include resin washed, injected dot, and moveable elements)? Rarity is a factor which can refer to a number of aspects including color and type of Bakelite, as well as the design itself. Figural jewelry, especially patriotic themes, command high prices in the collectibles market. Intricately reverse carved and painted pieces can cost several thousand dollars and are rare.

Apple juice colored Bakelite discs are topped by turquoise color beads and attached to a celluloid chain. This necklace makes quite a racket when worn. $400.00 – 600.00.

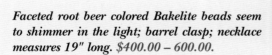

Faceted root beer colored Bakelite beads seem to shimmer in the light; barrel clasp; necklace measures 19" long. $400.00 – 600.00.

Marbled spinach-colored carved seashell pendant has a matching petite pin; matching screw-back earrings are not shown. The pendant measures 2" wide. Mounted on a simple link chain. The smell test worked by rubbing this piece; no hot water was required. $150.00 – 200.00 for all pieces.

Black Bakelite pendant features a non-Bakelite plastic cameo; celluloid chain. The pendant measures 3" wide. $150.00 – 200.00. To the right, Bakelite brooch measures 2¼" tall x 2" wide; plastic cameo. $75.00 – 125.00.

Two cameo pendants and one cameo brooch; only the upper right is mounted on a beautifully carved creamed corn color Bakelite; measures 2¾" tall x 2" wide. $125.00 – 175.00. Middle and left, reverse-carved Lucite and non-Bakelite cameos; pendant, $75.00 – 125.00, and brooch, $75.00 – 125.00.

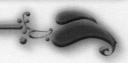

Carved Bakelite brooch measures 3" wide x 1½" deep; heat set pin back. $100.00 – 150.00.

Attributed to Martha Sleeper, this brooch features creamed corn colored Bakelite, floppy leather ears, carved and painted details. The brooch measures 2" tall x 1½" wide. Unsigned. $600.00 – 800.00.

The bongo player is metal but the drum is carved Bakelite. Unsigned. $50.00 – 75.00.

Bakelite vase is trimmed with painted wood sombreros; carved and paint details on the pot. Measures 2¼" tall. $200.00 – 300.00.

Carved, over-dyed Bakelite log with orange balls attached with plastic covered string. You can see the carving marks on the oranges; string has lost some of its plastic coating. $200.00 – 300.00.

Massive butterscotch colored Bakelite flower has a pierced center. Beautiful carving; heat set pin back; the brooch measures 3" in diameter. $300.00 – 400.00.

Top: beautiful Bakelite horse head brooch features brass bridle and glass eye; some carving; pin back is attached with rivets. $200.00 – 300.00.
Bottom: almost identical resin-washed horse head features brass bridle and glass eye. $200.00 – 300.00.

Creamed corn colored Bakelite Scottie brooch features paint details and glass eye. Brooch measures 3" long; pin back is attached with rivets. $300.00 – 400.00.

Bakelite dagger brooch features a marbled green handle with metal studs and chain accents. The blade is over-dyed and carved. The metal is not rusted; it appears to have been painted brown at one time. It measures 3¼" long. $400.00 – 500.00.

Heavily carved butterscotch colored Bakelite pendant is in the shape of a rose; there is some paint detail which is hard to see behind the flower. This is made entirely of Bakelite and measures 1½" wide. $100.00 – 150.00.

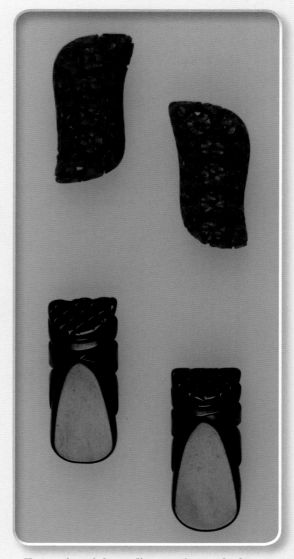

Backside of the carved clips; on the side less exposed to light, you can see the beautiful green color that these once were.

Two pairs of dress clips are featured; the top set is heavily carved in a repeating floral pattern and have darkened considerably through oxidation. On the backside you can see the much lighter shade of green that the clips were originally. $75.00 – 125.00.

The pair on the bottom are black carved Bakelite featuring a simple geometric design. While dress clips are not particularly rare, it's always a treat to find a matching pair. From the 1930s. $100.00 – 150.00.

Beautifully carved brooch with matching dress clips; even better than finding a set of matched clips is finding the matching brooch! Heat set pin back; the brooch measures 3" long x 1¾" wide; the dress clips measure 2" long. $150.00 – 200.00 set.

1930s root beer colored Bakelite belt buckle features a pleasing Art Deco design trimmed with colorful rhinestones. It measures 3¾" wide x 1¾". $125.00 – 175.00.

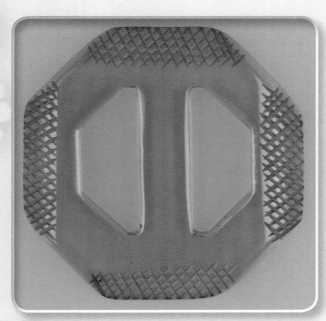

Apple juice colored belt buckle is very large and measures about 2¾" wide. It features a cross-hatch (slash-carved) design; 1930s. $100.00 – 150.00.

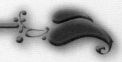

These narrow bangles are referred to as spacers and are shown in a variety of lovely colors. From a collectibles standpoint, they are not rare. But I like to wear about a dozen of them at a time á la Nancy Cunard. The noise lets everyone know you have arrived; and besides I love the way they look. *$15.00 – 30.00 each, depending on color.*

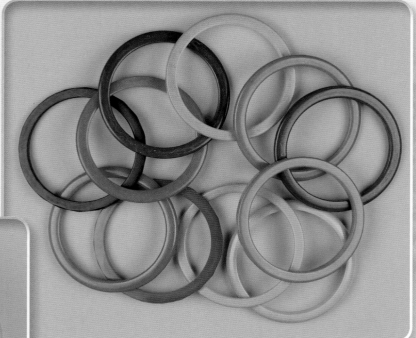

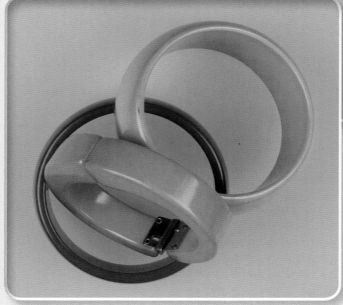

Smooth, creamed corn colored bangle (1" wide) and clamper are shown with a smooth creamed spinach colored bangle on bottom. Clamper measures about ½" wide; creamed spinach bangle measures ¾" wide. Bangles, *$100.00 – 150.00 each.* Clamper, *$150.00 – 200.00.*

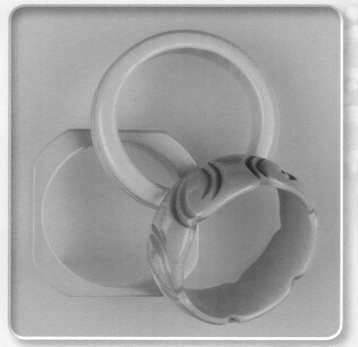

Three creamed corn colored bangles are shown; the bottom octagon-shaped bangle has no carving and measure 2½" wide, *$100.00 – 150.00;* next, simply carved bangle has two incised horizontal rows; it measures ¾" wide, *$125.00 – 175.00;* on top, more detail is shown in the carving on this bangle; it measures 1¼" wide, *$150.00 – 200.00.* These produce the Bakelite "thunk" when they come into contact with one another.

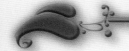 

Carved Bakelite bangles are featured in a trio of colors.
$75.00 – 100.00 each.

*Two examples of Mahjong bracelets; top, $100.00 –
150.00. On the bottom, larger pieces alternate with
black Bakelite rods. $150.00 – 200.00.*

*This bracelet features alternating black and white links; the
black and white pieces are glued together then attached to the
inner links with metal rods. Based on the color and smell, I
believe this bracelet is made from Galalith. $150.00 – 200.00.*
   *Note: When it was first produced, Catalin came in a wide
range of colors including white, pale blue, and lavender, among many other colors. These have mostly
disappeared today because of the oxidation
process that occurs over time. However it is
possible to find pieces which have been
packed away that retain their original
coloring.*

*Newer Bakelite bangle features over-
dyed surface; it is then carved back
to reveal the marbled color. These
were often sold with matching earrings.
Attributed to Diane Von Furstenberg; however, this is not signed. $100.00 – 150.00.*

Wire Jewelry

A few years ago I was browsing through an antique shop when I encountered my first piece of wire jewelry. I asked the shop owner about the bracelet I was looking at and she said, "oh, that's prison jewelry." Evidently her grandmother had done her share of crafts while doing time for bootlegging. That day I bought the bracelet and matching earrings as well as a wire ring while thinking that this jewelry had some interesting provenance. Many hours of research later, I have learned much about arts and crafts programs in prisons like San Quentin and Sing Sing. For example, the idea of providing cultural activity for inmates first began under the leadership of a visionary warden at San Quentin named Clinton Duffy in the 1930s. So are those portrait rings and wire bracelets really prison jewelry? Some are, some are not. Some were made in high school classes; some were made in reformatories and prisons. And some were probably mass produced as evidenced by the uniform workmanship.[17] Values for these pieces are based upon whether they were made by hand or mass produced. The more evidence of hand work, the greater the value to collectors of such pieces.

For whom was the jewelry made? In San Quentin, productive inmates could sell their jewelry in the prison store and keep a small percentage of the profits. When they were released, the money they accumulated helped them get a fresh, and hopefully honest, start. Mr. Duffy tells the story of one industrious inmate who actually started a plastics business when he left prison. He was the one who began making rings from his toothbrush while in solitary confinement. In the case of the bootlegging grandma, perhaps she made a few pieces for herself.

After my prison jewelry article was published I received several notes from folks whose fathers and grandfathers made jewelry during their incarceration as POWs in WWII. The jewelry was made from any scrap of metal or wood that a prisoner could find. Often working in secret, or to fill the long hours of boredom, prisoners labored to make a small gift for their beloved wife, sweetheart, mother, or daughter. The activity was much more than a way to pass the time; thoughts of a loved one provided a prisoner with a reason to live. Did it make a difference? According to Victor Frankel, a psychotherapist who survived life in a WWII concentration camp and wrote about it in his memoir, "Man's Search for Meaning," it often made the difference between living and dying.

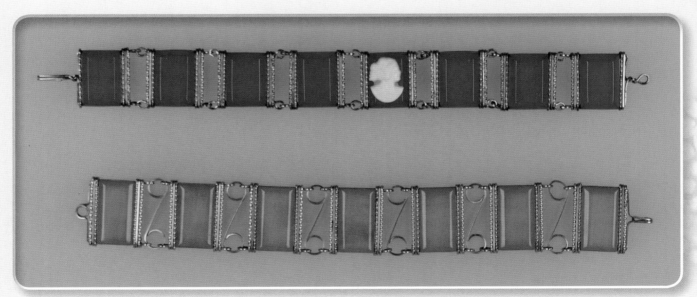

Top: Bracelet has evenly spaced plastic inserts in metal setting. The plastic cameo is glued on. $75.00 – 100.00.
Bottom: The metal on this bracelet is more irregularly shaped, suggesting that the inks were formed individually. Matching earrings are not shown. $100.00 – 125.00.

[17] Rehmann, Jacqueline. "Prison Jewelry: Is It or Isn't It?" *VFCJ*, Volume 19, No. 4, 2009.

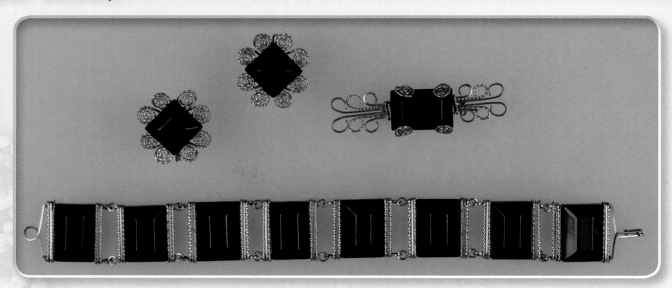

Black bracelet is made like the one on the previous page, with uniform metal links between the plastic inserts. *$75.00 – 100.00. The pin and earrings set features curlicue metal loops that are not uniform. The plastic inserts are held in place with "links" formed by taking metal from the back of the pieces and bringing it around to the front. Brooch measures almost 2" long; earrings measure 1" wide, including metal. $75.00 – 100.00.*

The green bracelet on top has fancy metal work which is obviously hand wrought. The ornate clasp is very unusual; the bracelet measures 7" long. $125.00 – 150.00.
On the bottom, the bracelet's plastic panels are connected by irregularly-shaped links. The clasp is a simple affair, two small hooks on one end which go through loops on the other. $125.00 – 150.00.

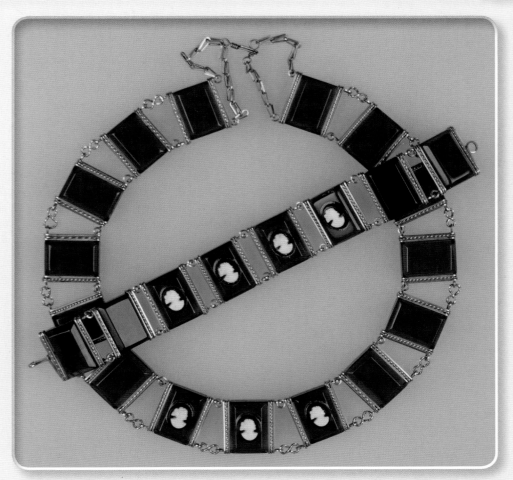

This well-made set features a cobalt blue necklace and bracelet. The necklace measures 15" long and lies flat on the neck when worn, the result of two links on the bottom and one link between the top inserts. The plastic cameos are evenly spaced on both the bracelet and necklace. Although beautiful, it lacks the hand wrought look of some of the other wire pieces. $175.00 – 225.00.

I purchased the upper ring at the shop described earlier. You can see the uniform wire setting; the stone is plastic and very lightweight. On the left, you can see the wire setting also; it is not as ornate as the other and features a simple loop design. $50.00 – 75.00 each.

Fun Plastics

Spanning the decades, the colorful plastic jewelry featured in these pages will certainly make you smile.

Silver charm bracelet (marked Sterling) has a variety of plastic charms that feature household products including DUZ laundry soap, Bab-O cleanser, Ritz crackers, and Lucky Strike cigarettes. The bracelet has a simple spring link clasp. $100.00 – 150.00.

Bright fuchsia-colored Lucite bangle has real beetles embedded in the plastic. This bracelet is reminiscent of the Victorian fad for making jewelry with real insects. From the 1960s, unsigned. $250.00 – 300.00.

This tutti frutti bracelet from the 1960s features lightweight plastic discs with matching clip earrings. $40.00 – 65.00 set.

Marbled hearts contrast with the chunky darker green plastic links in this 1970s bracelet. Each heart measures 1½" x 1½". $35.00 – 50.00.

Double strand choker length necklace features green and orange pineapples. The palm trees were probably a later addition to the earrings. $50.00 – 75.00.

Plastic fruits and flowers adorn this festive necklace; large beads are faceted and sparkle like real crystals. Unsigned. $100.00 – 150.00.

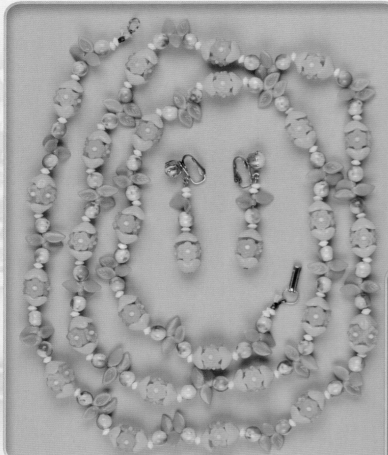

Colorful floral necklace and earrings are signed "Hong Kong;" the soft plastic is very lightweight. Necklace measures 48" long! $50.00 – 75.00 set.

Set is featured with multicolored beads, this time with matching bracelet. Signed "HONG KONG." $75.00 – 100.00.

Molded roses in pale yellow and coral colors are accented with both clear and green leaves on this necklace that measures 20" long. The paperweight beads in between look like glass but are lightweight plastic. Signed "Made in West Germany" on the pretty clasp. $50.00 – 75.00.

1960s Mod-style necklace measures 22" long and was made in West Germany. $50.00 – 75.00.

The moveable figure on this brooch measures 5" tall; this lady looks like a flapper — note the flapper-style headdress. Polystyrene plastic. $100.00 – 150.00.

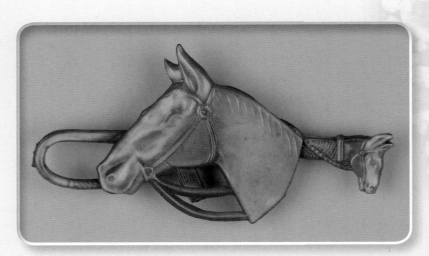

Popular horse brooches were made in plastics and wood; sometimes the same design surfaced in both. Here is a molded plastic horse head with a detailed riding crop. $35.00 – 50.00.

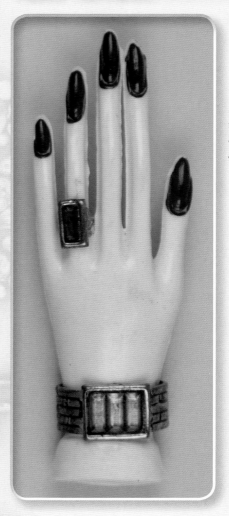

1940s molded plastic hand brooch measures 2¾" long; the ring and bracelet are made of metal. $50.00 – 75.00.

Brooch features a moonshine jug and out-house. Novelty jewelry from the 1920s and 1930s were generally inexpensive trinkets that were made with a touch of humor. These were sold in five-and-ten-cent stores. $25.00 – 40.00.

La Conga was a popular 1930s night-club located in New York City; the term can also refer to the dance in which participants form a long line (Conga line) that snakes around the dance floor to the beat of Latin music. This pin is made of painted hard plastic. $25.00 – 40.00.

Pearlized plastic brooch is very dimensional and mea-sures 4" in diameter; note the pink pearl centers in the flowers. $50.00 – 75.00.

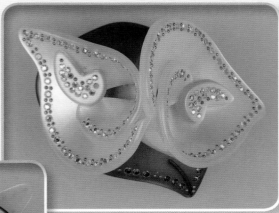

The hardware on this brooch suggests that it is a newer piece. It features a perennial favorite, calla lilies. $35.00 – 50.00.

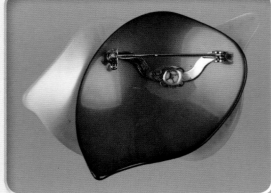

Detail of calla lily brooch showing newer style clasp.

Hard plastic leaves dangle from a pretty pink branch on this brooch; celluloid chain supports the leaves. $35.00 – 50.00.

Detail of pin back shows older hardware, celluloid chain.

Although some of the components might resemble Bakelite, they aren't. Plastic leaves and chain make this a lightweight brooch even though it measures 4" long. $50.00 – 75.00.

Early coral and orange colored brooch features hard plastic and brass components. The orange plastic beads are hand wired onto a small perforated metal disc. The brooch measures 3¾ " long. $35.00 – 50.00.

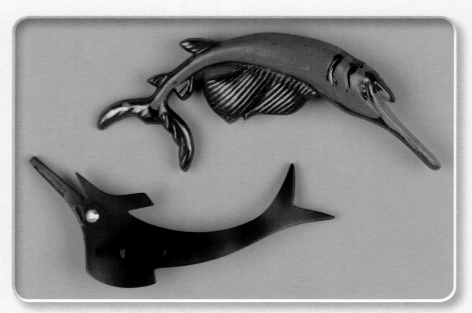

Playful plastic fish brooches; the top features painted details and pearlescence finish. $35.00 – 50.00. Bottom is faux tortoise with rhinestone eye. $25.00 – 40.00.

Clear plastic swordfish brooch features painted details. $35.00 – 50.00. Donkey brooch has moveable legs and twine tail; he can actually stand up, albeit precariously. $25.00 – 40.00; lower left chatelaine features mother and baby penguin with painted details. $50.00 – 75.00; and the Heinz pickle pin is made from hard plastic. $25.00 – 40.00.

A variety of molded plastic figures are depicted on the brooches here; at the top an ice skater, perhaps the popular Sonya Henie; next, a figure that reminds me of Lou Costello from Laurel and Hardy; lower left, a promotional pin advertising Revlon cosmetics; and lower right, a covered wagon. $25.00 – 40.00 each.

Colorful owl brooch is marked "Made in WGermany"; it measures 2¾" high; "Butch" and the playful elephant (Dumbo perhaps?) are molded plastic. $25.00 – 40.00 each.

Brooch with molded birds is made of celluloid; the trio is marked "JAPAN." $45.00 – 60.00; single bird pin is unsigned. $25.00 – 40.00.

Colorful molded plastic figures on these brooches are marked "Czechoslovakia" on the metal pin back. $50.00 – 75.00 each.

Top: *Molded celluloid brooch with Scotties is marked "Occupied Japan" on the metal pin back. $40.00 – 65.00.*
Bottom: *Popular Scottie dogs were made in a variety of materials including Bakelite and other plastics as well as wood. If this pin were made of Bakelite, the value would be much higher. $25.00 – 50.00.*

Left: *Whimsical plastic elephant tusk supports red plastic elephants on this brooch. $35.00 – 60.00.*
Right: *Saddle with riding boots is another motif that appeared on brooches in a variety of materials including wood, Bakelite, and other plastics. $35.00 – 60.00.*

The plastic ice skates of this brooch feature fur trim and paint detail on the skate blades to mimic metal. $50.00 – 75.00.

The hat brooch on the left is celluloid, $35.00 – 60.00; the lightweight sombrero pin on the right features a plastic covered string accent. $35.00 – 60.00.

Popular horse and buggy brooch was designed by Nicholas Barbieri for Uncas Manufacturing; the design patent was issued on September 29, 1942; the patent number appears on the brooch (133919). $50.00 – 75.00.

Playful pin made of molded plastic; looks like this fellow has celebrated a little too heartily. $25.00 – 40.00.

Graceful reindeer pin is marked with a number (6410) but is otherwise unsigned. Measures 3½" in length. $35.00 – 60.00.

The pair of playful elephants featured on this brooch have carved and painted details. $50.00 – 75.00.

Popular wartime eagle motif is featured on this pin in molded moonglow plastic with rhinestone trim. $100.00 – 125.00.

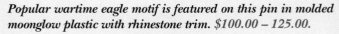

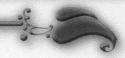

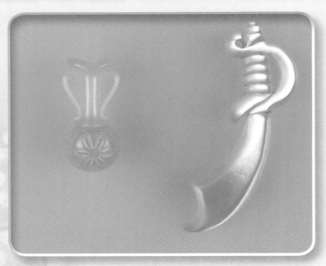

The petite vase brooch on the left can hold water; women would wear it with a real flower; measures 1¾" tall. $25.00 – 40.00.
Moonglow saber pin on the right measures 3½" long. $35.00 – 50.00.

Painted plastic bunny brooch is made in three pieces and measures 1¾" x 2¼" long. $50.00 – 75.00.

Musical themes are depicted in these plastic brooches.
Left: Guitar, $25.00 – 40.00.
Right: Musical note, $25.00 – 40.00.

Mod design brooches with black ring accents; each measures 3¼" long. $50.00 – 75.00 each.

Lucite Jewelry

Acrylic plastics were developed in Germany by Dr. Otto Rohm whose company (Rohm & Haas) introduced Plexiglas® in 1931. In 1937 the Du Pont company introduced their acrylic product which they named Lucite. Today, whether it is Plexiglas or Lucite, most acrylic jewelry is referred to as Lucite.

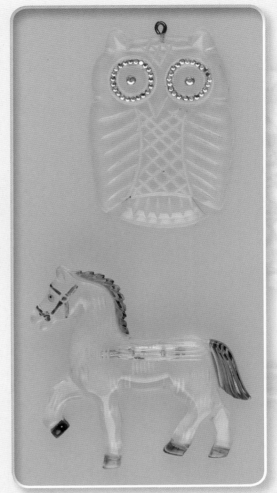

Top: Lucite owl pendant has crystal clear rhinestones encircling its eyes; it measures 2½" tall x 1¾" wide; some carving. $50.00 – 75.00.
Bottom: Large prancing horse brooch has reverse carving and paint accents; it measures 2¾" x 2¾". $150.00 – 200.00.

Lucite sword pin features reverse carving; it measures 3½" long. $100.00 – 150.00.

Left: Frosted Lucite brooch features a molded leaf in silver tone setting; measures 2¾" tall x 1¾" wide; signed "LISNER." $50.00 – 75.00.
Right: Clever brooch features tongs holding a block of ice; it measures 2½" tall x 1¾" wide. $50.00 – 75.00.

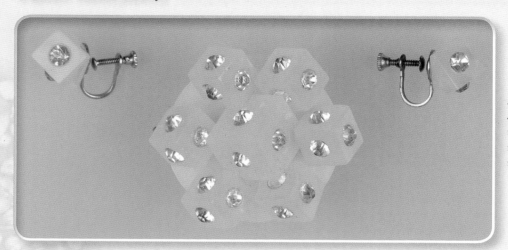

Lucky dice are decorated with pretty rhinestones in this frosted Lucite brooch with matching screw-back earrings; the brooch measures 1¾" in diameter; the earrings measure ½" each. $50.00 – 75.00.

Lucite Mother brooch has a white plastic backing and features reverse carving and painting. $35.00 – 60.00.

Two Lucite reverse-carved and painted brooches; the top one was made in a high school industrial arts class in the early 1950s. $45.00 – 50.00 each.

Reverse-carved, Lucite pendant features swimming fish; note the tiny bubble detail. Measuring 1½" wide, this piece is unsigned. $100.00 – 150.00.

Lucite fish bowl with goldfish pendant; a marvelous design that collectors love. The attached chain measures 24" long; unsigned. $150.00 – 200.00.

Vendôme choker features large frosted and clear Lucite beads with silver filigree caps; the matching earrings are not signed. $150.00 – 200.00 set.

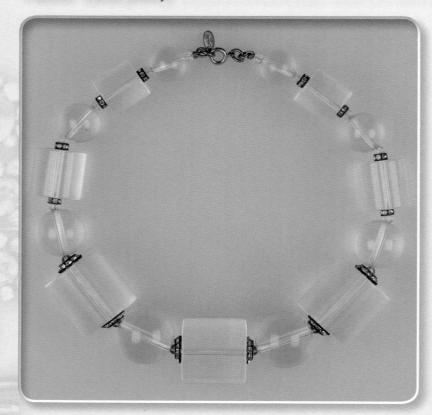

Chunky Lucite beads and cylinders are featured in this choker length necklace from Cadoro; signed with a hang tag. $100.00 – 150.00.

Frosted Lucite beads are accented with crystal clear rhinestones which dangle from a central chain. The grape leaf at the top is encrusted with clear rhinestones; snake chain; unsigned; the pendant measures 3" long. $100.00 – 150.00.

Mod-style pendant on gold-tone snake chain is signed "LANVIN Paris©;" the chain has the LANVIN "L" hang tag. The pendant measures 2½" long x 2" wide. Lanvin is the oldest continuing couture house in Paris. In the 1960s the company went through a dramatic makeover and introduced a less expensive, ready-to-wear line. After the makeover, the company produced a series of carved Op Art plastic pendants on chains which have become highly collectible. $400.00 – 600.00.

Gold-tone Leo the Lion is mounted on a Lucite pendant; it features a heavy 24" chain. Signed "ART©." $50.00 – 75.00.

Faceted Lucite is featured in this necklace by Avon. Marked with a paper hang tag only, the 26" long necklace features rondelle spacers and a barrel clasp. $35.00 – 50.00.

Colorful, faceted Lucite beads from the 1960s are featured in this pretty pastel necklace. Necklace features silver tone spacers; beads are graduated in size. Unsigned. $50.00 – 75.00.

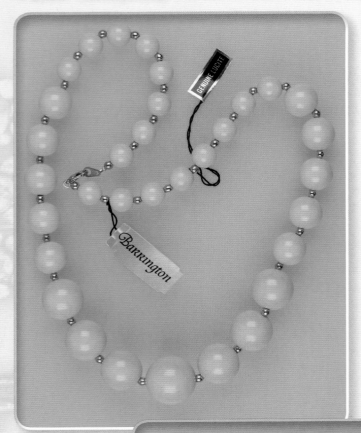

Opaque lilac-colored Lucite is marked with a paper hang tag, "Genuine Lucite." The 24" necklace sold for $16.00 when it was first introduced; price today, $35.00 – 60.00.

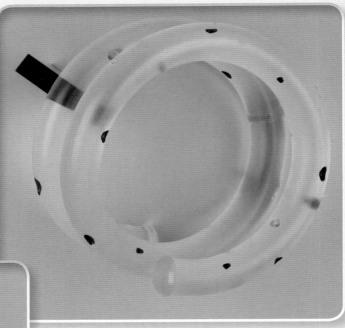

Wrap bracelet in lightly frosted Lucite features paint details. Unsigned. $50.00 – 75.00.

1940s Lucite bracelet is trimmed with real seashells; matching shell earrings are also shown. This type of jewelry is very fragile. Unsigned. $50.00 – 75.00 set.

Miriam Haskell Lucite bracelet with matching ear-rings features faceted crystals and rondelle spacers; the earrings are signed in two places; bracelet is marked with a metal hang tag. $175.00 – 225.00 set.

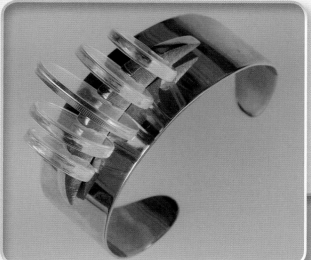

"Mod"-style cuff features discs of Lucite mounted onto the metal bracelet. Unsigned. $75.00 – 125.00.

Breathtaking parure by Boucher features adjustable necklace, brooch, bracelet, and matching earrings in shiny silver tone. The frosted Lucite leaves are trimmed with crystal clear rhinestones and baguettes; all pieces are signed "BOUCHER©" with the design number. $400.00 – 600.00.

Lea Stein

The jewelry and accessories of Lea Stein are made by layering 200 – 300 cellulose acetate sheets which are then baked to produce the beautiful designs shown in this section. Lea's husband, Fernand Steinberger, is credited with discovering the process for laminating celluloid which is the hallmark of Lea Stein components. Beginning in the 1960s, the company produced hair combs, bracelets, beaded necklaces, brooches and earrings, jewel boxes, purse mirrors, belt buckles, and buttons. Following a brief hiatus in the 1980s the company began making jewelry again and continues to this day. Among the earliest and most collectible designs are the serigraphy pins which depict Art Deco motifs including 1920s era women.

Indian head brooch (1968 – 1980) measures 2⅛" long. $125.00 – 175.00.

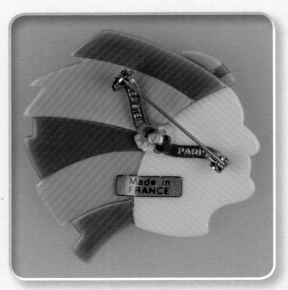

Brooches were signed "Lea Stein" and "Paris" on the characteristic v-shaped metal pin back as seen in this photograph, which is the backside of the previous Indian head pin. Less commonly seen is the "Made in France" sticker.

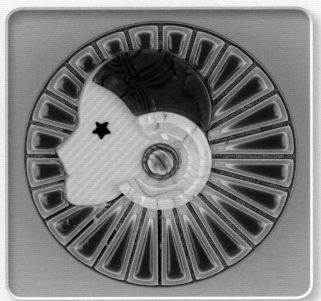

Dramatic "Colerette" brooch (1968 – 1980) measures 2¼" in diameter. $125.00 – 175.00.

Majestic bird has a ruby red background with gold covering. Made between 1968 and 1980, this brooch measures 2½" tall and has an applied plastic eye. $150.00 – 200.00.

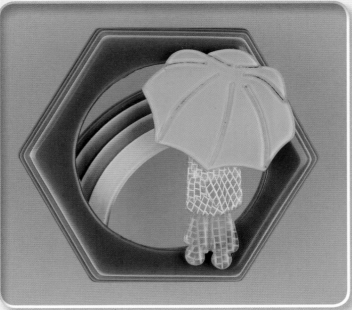

Rainbow and umbrella pin dates 1968 – 1980 and measures just 1½" wide. $100.00 – 150.00.

Dimensional and multicolored tortoise measures 3⅜" long. The tortoise brooches were first made in the 1990s. $75.00 – 125.00.

Pleasing parrot pin (1968 – 1980) measures 3½" tall. $100.00 – 150.00.

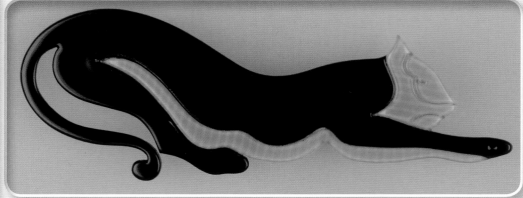

Graceful "pouncing panther" pin in plum and pink measures almost 4½" long. This design was made between 1968 and 1980. $125.00 – 175.00.

Plouc the dog pin in black and white measures 2" tall. $100.00 – 150.00.

Large butterfly has a wingspan of 3"; this pin features a marbled turquoise and red design. $100.00 – 150.00.

The most popular of Lea Stein designs is the three-dimensional fox. This brooch has a subtle harlequin pattern. These are made in many different colors and patterns. $100.00 – 150.00.

Double edelweiss features a pleasing color combination of purple, pink, green, and turquoise. This large, multilayered brooch measures almost 4" tall. $125.00 – 175.00.

Mid-Century Plastic Jewelry

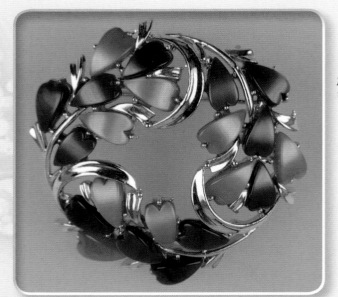

Taupe and tan plastic inserts are featured on this Coro circle pin. It measures 2" in diameter. The Coro signature is barely visible. $35.00 – 50.00.

A plastic disk does a fine job of serving as this turtle's shell. Unsigned. $25.00 – 40.00.

Matching pin and earrings are featured in autumn colors; small smoked topaz chatons add sparkle. It's easy to see why collectors love this jewelry; the plastic leaves seem to glow from within. All pieces are signed "LISNER©." $75.00 – 125.00.

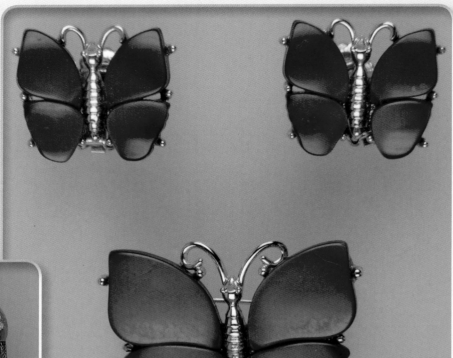

Cherry red butterfly brooch and matching earrings are unsigned. The pin measures 1¾" wide; the earrings measure 1" wide. $35.00 – 50.00.

Signed "Selro," this brooch and matching earrings feature white faces. Brushed gold-tone helmets have dangling chain detail. $200.00 – 250.00.

The plastic panels on this bracelet sparkle with embedded multicolored "confetti." The panels are wide and measure 1¼". Unsigned. $35.00 – 50.00.

Napier charm bracelets are favorites among collectors and it is easy to see why. This well-made example features brightly colored plastic balls and lustrous faux pearls. The beads are strung on sturdy wire and the clasp is signed "NAPIER." $150.00 – 250.00.

Faceted Lucite gives the illusion of crystals in these two charm bracelets. If they were made of glass the bracelets would be much too heavy to wear. Both are unsigned. $25.00 – 40.00 each.

Top: Faux marbled scarabs are featured in this lightweight link bracelet with matching earrings from Karu Arke. Just the bracelet is signed on the fold-over clasp. $45.00 – 60.00.

Bottom: Tiny seashells and glitter are embedded in huge chunks of clear plastic in this unsigned bracelet and matching earrings. Links measure 1¼" wide. $45.00 – 60.00.

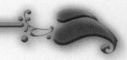

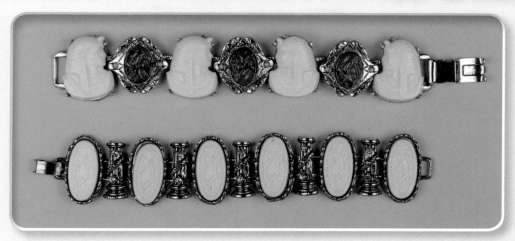

Top: Faux ivory Egyptian heads alternate with plastic scarabs in this Egyptian revival bracelet. Unsigned. $100.00 – 150.00.

Bottom: Classic figures adorn the faux ivory panels on this beautiful bracelet accented with turquoise and amethyst colored rhinestones. The plating is in excellent condition on both of these bracelets, which is not always the case on these pieces. Unsigned. $50.00 – 75.00.

Top: Faux grapes are accented with paint details and amethyst colored rhinestones on this five-link bracelet. Unsigned. $35.00 – 50.00.

Bottom: Bubble gum pink flowers are accented with gold-tone centers in this unsigned bracelet with matching earrings. The flowers measure 1½" wide. $35.00 – 50.00.

Top: Lavender colored flowers are accented with pretty purple chatons in this bracelet; matching earrings; unsigned. $35.00 – 50.00.
Middle: A lovely bracelet signed "B.S.K." features iridescent white and lilac leaves accented with aurora borealis chatons alternating with white enameled flowers. $50.00 – 75.00.
Bottom: Unsigned bracelet features lavender colored panels in a gold-tone setting. $35.00 – 50.00.

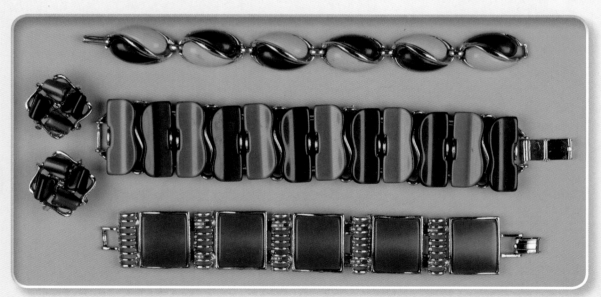

Top: Turquoise and brown comma-shaped inserts are featured in this unsigned bracelet. $35.00 – 50.00.
Middle: Forest green panels alternate with lighter green in this unsigned bracelet. It measures 1¼" wide and has coordinating earrings. $50.00 – 75.00.
Bottom: Tempting teal colored panels adorn this lovely gold-tone mid-century bracelet. Unsigned. $35.00 – 50.00.

Top: Olivine colored inserts are featured in this bracelet by ART. The matching earrings are also signed "ART©." $60.00 – 85.00.

Bottom: Surprisingly unsigned, this high quality bracelet features hearts and flowers with gold-tone accents. It measures ¾" wide. $50.00 – 75.00; higher if signed.

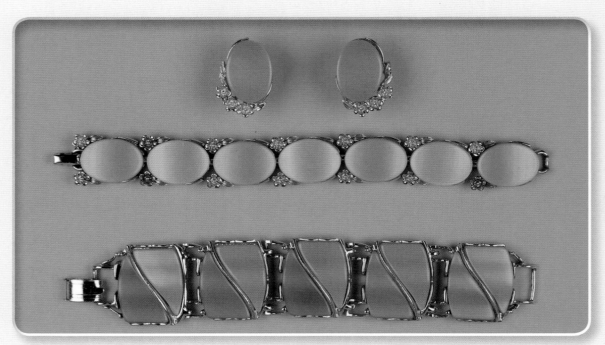

Top: Unsigned orange and yellow bracelet has matching earrings set in gold-tone with fold-over clasp. $35.00 – 50.00.

Bottom: Pale yellow and taupe panels are set into shiny gold-tone on this bracelet, which measures 1¼" wide; unsigned. $35.00 – 50.00.

Top: Pearly cream colored plastic discs in a shiny gold setting; unsigned. $25.00 – 40.00.
Bottom: Creamy orbs are featured in this bracelet by Coro. $45.00 – 60.00.

Top: Figural bracelet which is often referred to as "Thai girl." This well-made bracelet is attributed to Selini. $100.00 – 150.00.
Middle: Mesh bracelet features faux stones. Signed "SARAHCOV." $45.00 – 60.00.
Bottom: Fancy filigree setting is featured in this faux stone bracelet. Unsigned. $35.00 – 40.00.

This bracelet is signed "SELINI©." $100.00 – 150.00.

The backs of the plastic faces are stamped "SELINI©" in this link bracelet with matching earrings. The wide bracelet measures 1¾" x 7¾" long. $300.00 – 400.00 set.

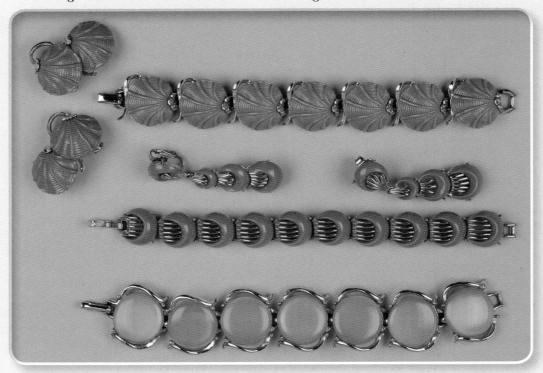

Top: Coral colored seashells are featured in this pretty bracelet with matching earrings. Signed "Lisner©." $60.00 – 85.00.
Middle: Trifari bracelet with matching dangle earrings; the earrings measure 2¼" long; all pieces are marked. $75.00 – 100.00.
Bottom: Coral colored disks seem to glow from within in this pretty bracelet. Unsigned. $35.00 – 50.00.

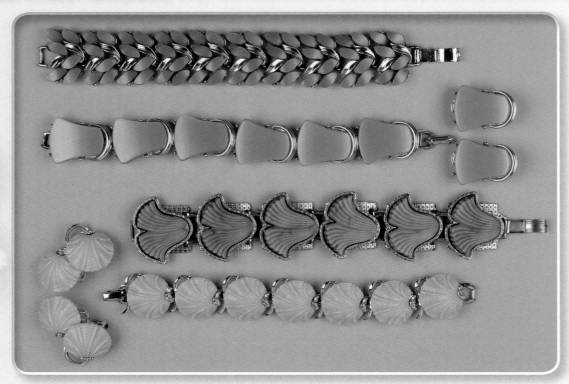

Top: Tiny leaves adorn this pretty aqua colored bracelet; signed "CLAUDETTE©." $75.00 – 100.00.
Second from top: Unusually-shaped plastic panels are featured in this unsigned bracelet with matching earrings. $50.00 – 75.00.
Third from top: Variegated scallop panels are set into pretty silver tone; unsigned. $25.00 – 40.00.
Bottom: Lisner shell design matches the coral bracelet shown previously; this bracelet also has matching earrings. Signed "LISNER©." $60.00 – 85.00.

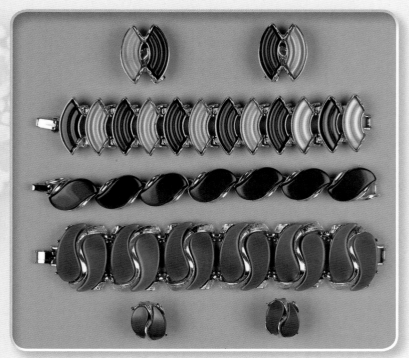

Top: Alternating navy blue and gray plastic inserts adorn this silver-tone bracelet with matching earrings. Unsigned. $50.00 – 75.00.
Middle: Navy blue swirls decorate this silver-tone bracelet, signed "LISNER©." $45.00 – 60.00.
Bottom: I would call this color periwinkle; wide unsigned bracelet measures 1½" and has matching earrings. Gorgeous. $50.00 – 75.00.

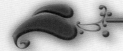

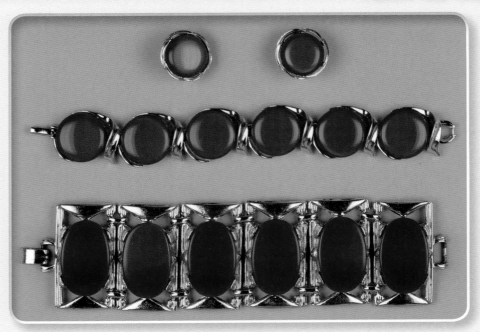

Top: Cherry red orbs are featured in this pretty bracelet with matching earrings by *LISNER©*. $60.00 – 85.00.
Bottom: Wide is the word for this pretty *PAM©* bracelet that measures 2" in width. $45.00 – 60.00.

Top: This bracelet is the same design as the navy blue one shown previously; this one is also by *LISNER©*. $45.00 – 60.00.
Bottom: Pretty filigree findings are accented with cherry red inserts on this bracelet. Matching earrings, unsigned. $65.00 – 80.00.

Anyone want to cha cha? This is one festive bracelet! With matching clip earrings; each turquoise and white bead is attached to metal discs with a link so they move freely. Unsigned. $75.00 – 100.00.

Pretty expansion bracelets feature different designs. Pink is by Trifari and measures 1¼" wide, $50.00 – 75.00; blue bracelet is unsigned and measures 1½" wide, $35.00 – 60.00; the red one reminds me of licorice and measures 2" wide, unsigned, $35.00 – 60.00.

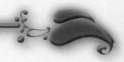

In the following photographs, Weiss plastic bracelets are featured in a variety of colors. Some are signed, others are not. Originally sold in the 1950s, these bracelets were featured in dozens of color combinations. Matching earrings were often included and sometimes it is only the earrings in a set that are signed.

Baby blue with blue and crystal clear rhinestones. Signed "WEISS" on the metal hinge. $125.00 – 175.00.

Lemon yellow bracelet is not signed. $100.00 – 150.00.

Bracelet with marbled effect with clear rhinestones is not signed. $100.00 – 150.00.

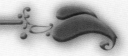

The colorful chatons sparkle beautifully in this bracelet, signed "WEISS." $125.00 – 175.00.

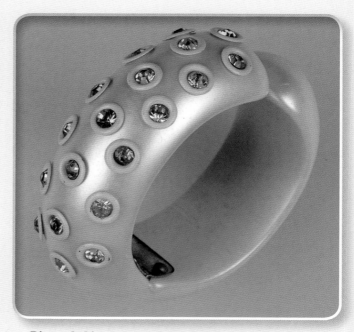

Rimmed rhinestones and pearlescence give this bracelet a different look. Unsigned. $125.00 – 175.00.

This beauty features paint details and aurora borealis rhinestones. You can see the hinge is set into the plastic. $150.00 – 200.00.

Rows and rows of crystal clear rhinestones contrast beautifully with the black background; unsigned. $125.00 – 175.00.

This magnificent clamper really sparkles on the wrist. Signed "WEISS." $125.00 – 175.00.

This beauty is signed "WEISS" and features large and small chatons for maximum sparkle. $125.00 – 175.00.

Paint details and rhinestones clustered like flowers are beautiful in this unsigned black bracelet. $150.00 – 200.00.

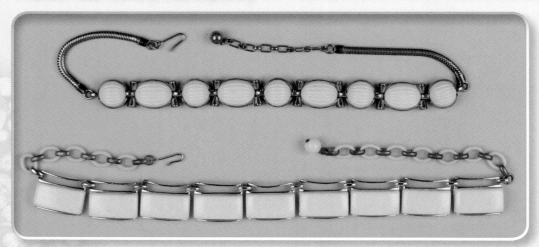

Top: Pretty pink serrated cabochons are featured in this necklace with snake chain and fish hook clasp. This sturdy and well made necklace is signed "TRIFARI©" on the inside of the fish hook clasp. I almost missed it except I have seen this necklace in vintage ads (See Figure 44). $45.00 – 60.00.

Bottom: Necklace reminds me of pink Chiclets; note the plastic links on the chain. Signed "LISNER©." $35.00 – 50.00.

Figure 44: Trifari advertisement featuring the Brazil collar, bracelet, and two different styles of matching earrings.

For Her... Jewels by TRIFARI®

Left to right: Top row—VALENCIA* Collar, 7.50; Bracelet, 5.00; Earrings, 4.00. COLLEEN Collar, 7.50; Bracelet, 5.00; Earrings, 5.00; BASKET PIN, 7.50; PEBBLE BEACH* Collar, 5.00; Bracelet, 4.00; Earrings, 4.00. Center–FLEURETTES* Pin, 5.00; Button Earrings, 6.00. Bottom Row–BRAZIL* Collar, 7.50; Half Collar (not shown), 5.00; Bracelet, 5.00; Button Earrings, 3.00; Drop Earrings, 4.00. FLEURETTES* Collar, 7.50; Bracelet, 6.00; Contour Earrings, 4.00. TRINIDAD Collar, 6.00; Bracelet, 5.00; Earrings, 4.00.

Prices plus tax. Jewelry designs copyrighted. Not authentic unless stamped Trifari. *Also in colors.

Somewhere in my house are matching earrings for this pretty purple and fuchsia necklace. Signed "Coro©." $45.00 – 60.00.

All three necklaces are signed "Coro©;" the inner one has plastic petals and crystal clear rhinestone centers in the dazzling flowers, $45.00 – 60.00, because it has matching earrings (not shown); the next two are almost identical in color; only the design of the metal components differs. $35.00 – 50.00 each.

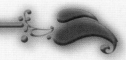

*Iridescent jelly leaves accented with aurora borealis chatons are featured in this lovely set from **LISNER**©. $65.00 – 80.00.*

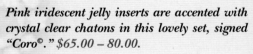

Pink iridescent jelly inserts are accented with crystal clear chatons in this lovely set, signed "Coro©." $65.00 – 80.00.

Upper right: Shimmering brown half moons are featured in this necklace by LISNER©. $35.00 – 50.00.

Middle: Pretty aqua colored necklace matches the pink one shown on page 94. They are the same length, with the difference being in the number of cabochons in the necklace. Also signed "TRIFARI©" on the inside of the clasp. $45.00 – 60.00.

Lower left: Faux turquoise cabochons are completed by the silver tone setting in this unsigned necklace. $25.00 – 40.00.

Alternating shades of green are complemented with tiny aurora borealis cabochons on the outer edge of the leaves on the necklace and earrings, signed "LISNER©." $100.00 – 125.00.

Cherries, bananas, green apples, and pears fit together nicely in this yummy necklace with matching earrings. The 24" chain is designed to slip over the wearer's head. Unsigned. $50.00 – 75.00.

Real shells are set into the plastic pendant and earrings; unsigned. $50.00 – 75.00.

Baby blue Bogoff necklace with matching earrings is accented with crystal clear chatons. All pieces, including clip earrings are signed "BOGOFF©." $50.00 – 75.00.

Classic satinore necklace and memory bracelet are by Richelieu but unsigned. This color is called Angel Pink. The 1946 ad in Figure 45 shows a set in the color Star Sapphire. The necklace has a tiny push-in clasp. Unsigned. $50.00 – 75.00.

Figure 45: Richelieu Satinore advertisement featuring a double strand necklace, matching memory bracelet, brooch, and two styles of earrings. Other colors included Moonstone, Star Ruby, Star Sapphire (featured in ad), Angel Pink, and Chalcedony, "which radiates elusive light rays." The ad is dated November 3, 1948.

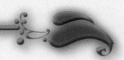

*Earrings and circle brooch from the Iridelle collection.
$35.00 – 50.00.*

*Richelieu Iridelle translucent bead necklace and
memory bracelet are featured in this photograph.
This type of jewelry was popular in the late 1940s
and early 1950s. Other pieces in the set included earrings and circle brooch. Unsigned. $75.00 – 125.00.*

*Irregularly shaped pearls are featured in this lovely set
by B.S.K. Matching earrings are also signed. $40.00
– 65.00.*

Lovely Lisner set features an antiqued gold-tone setting with faux crackle beads in pastel colors. Only the earrings are signed. $65.00 – 80.00.

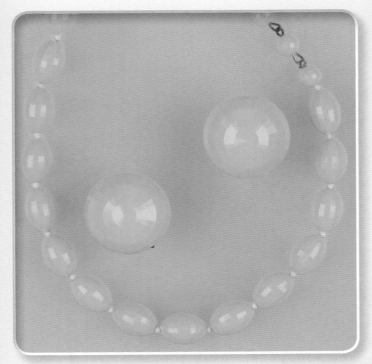

Bubble gum pink necklace is made with faceted plastic beads and measures a scant 15½" long. Only the matching clip earrings are signed "Dalsheim." $35.00 – 50.00.

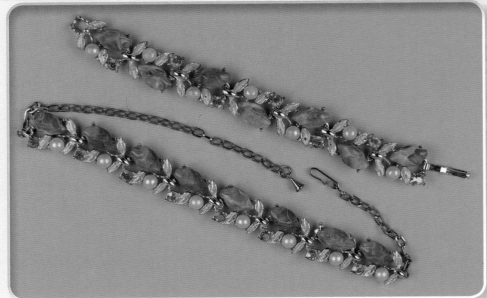

Unsigned bracelet and necklace features blue, irregularly-haped plastic stones with aurora borealis and faux pearl accents in a shiny silver-tone setting. $65.00 – 80.00.

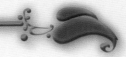

Feathery shapes in a bright shade of neon coral are combined with crystal clear chatons in this necklace and matching earrings by TRIFARI©. The clip earrings are large and measure 1½" at widest. $65.00 – 80.00.

Ruby red swirl inserts are pretty in this necklace and brooch signed "STAR©." Silver-tone setting. $50.00 – 75.00.

Pretty coral colored petals are featured in this matching necklace, brooch, and clip earrings. The brooch is large and measures 2¼" x 1½". Signed "KRAMER©." $100.00 – 125.00.

Popular with collectors, this jelly leaf-shaped gold-tone bracelet, necklace, and screw-back earrings are signed "LISNER©." $150.00 – 175.00.

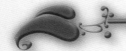

Soft plastic flowers are accented with tiny pearls, and citrine and topaz colored chatons in this lovely set by ART©. All pieces are signed. $100.00 – 125.00.

Olive green married set includes brooch with matching pierced earrings, necklace, and ring. All are unsigned. Brooch with matching earrings, $45.00 – 60.00; necklace, $25.00 – 40.00, and ring, $25.00 – 40.00.

Featherweight set in pale pink features matching bracelet, earrings, and necklace. Each flower is accented with a crystal clear chaton. Lovely. $40.00 – 65.00.

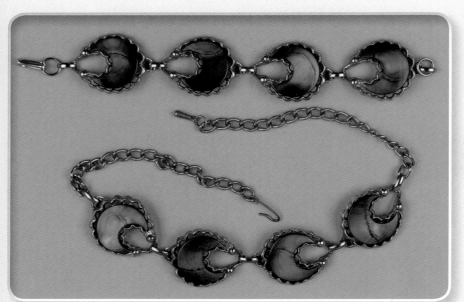

Marbled gray crescents are featured in this matching bracelet and necklace. Unsigned. $40.00 – 65.00.

105

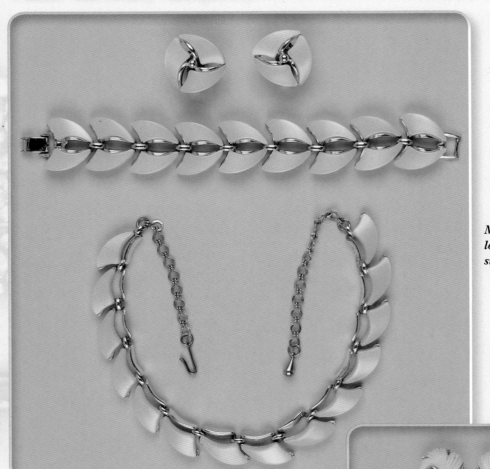

Moonglow plastic inserts are featured in this lovely set by Claudette. Only the earrings are signed. $100.00 – 125.00.

Trifari set is featured in pink and white. Note that this is the same feather motif as seen in the neon coral bracelet and earrings shown on page 102. All pieces are signed "TRIFARI©." $175.00 – 225.00.

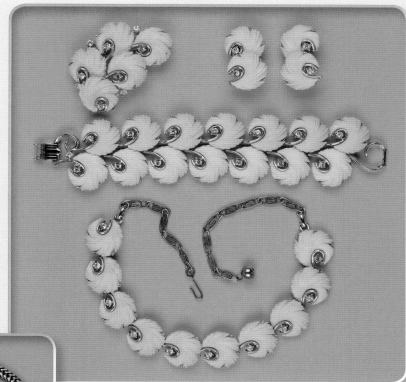

The same Trifari set shown on the previous page, but featured in white. $125.00 – 150.00.

Red Selro faces are featured in this bolo-style necklace, brooch, and matching earrings. All pieces are signed "SELRO©." A very desirable set in a great color. $400.00 – 600.00.

Detail of Selro brooch.

White devil set is unsigned. This design has been attributed to ART and Florenza. $200.00 – 250.00.

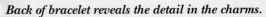

Back of bracelet reveals the detail in the charms.

Striking necklace and bracelet from Charel features golden topaz stones and confetti cabochons. Both pieces are signed. $150.00 – 200.00.

Egyptian inspired parure features faux jade and coral accents with gold-tone figures. This lovely set is unsigned. $200.00 – 250.00.

Beads and More Beads

Plastic beaded jewelry is a perennial favorite. In the early 1960s women layered several strands under suits and over sweaters (See Figure 46). The size belies the weight of these wonderful accessories which are often surprisingly light-weight. Examples spanning several decades are shown below.

Molded red rose beads are strung on string; plastic leaves are interspersed throughout. The mold lines are visible on most beads. Unsigned. $50.00 – 75.00.

Figure 46: Triple strand beaded necklace provides just the right touch to this suit made from Du Pont nylon and metallic yarn. Ad is from November 1962, *Mademoiselle* **magazine.**

Early unsigned necklace features plastic beads with multicolored caps on a plastic chain; simple spring link clasp. Attributed to Miriam Haskell. $200.00 – 300.00.

Pale peach pearls are interspersed with opaque and clear beads with smooth and mottled surfaces. Signed "GERMANY" on the fishhook clasp. *$35.00 – 50.00.*

Festive bib-style necklace features faceted plastic beads in various shapes and colors; signed, but I cannot make out the signature. $35.00 – 60.00.

Detailed bib-style necklace features orange and white beads, some with a marbled effect. Unsigned. $50.00 – 75.00.

Shimmering smooth beads are featured in this pretty necklace from Monet; signed with a metal hang tag. $40.00 – 65.00.

Five-strand necklace features plastic beads of various sizes and a beautiful metal clasp with enameled flower trim. Signed "SELINI©." $75.00 – 125.00.

Adjustable double-strand necklace features large, faceted plastic beads, and fish hook clasp. Signed "WGERMANY" on the clasp. $35.00 – 50.00.

Four-strand adjustable necklace features evenly sized, faceted orange and yellow beads with gold filigree caps; a few iridescent spaces add extra sparkle in this piece. Signed "WestGermany." $35.00 – 50.00.

Lightweight five-strand necklace features faceted beads; this also has filigree caps and iridescent spacers. Signed "WestGermany." $35.00 – 50.00.

Irregularly-shaped glitter beads are featured in this lightweight necklace. Some are opaque, others translucent. Signed *"KRAMER." $50.00 – 75.00.*

From Eisenberg Ice comes this lovely purple three-strand necklace. The clasp is richly decorated with prong set chatons. It flips up and the beads are connected on a hook inside; that is also where the signature cartouche is located. *$75.00 – 100.00.*

The 1960s and Onward

The popularity of plastics for use in costume jewelry only continued to grow. Size and color were two major reasons; big jewelry was still extremely lightweight and the colors were vibrant and beautiful.

This floral brooch features soft plastic petals that are accented with aurora borealis rhinestones; they look like raindrops on the petals. Only the earrings are signed "Vendome©." The large brooch measures 4¼" tall; the flower is 1½" deep and 2" in diameter. $150.00 – 200.00.

The Vendome brooch is featured here in pale blue with silver-tone setting. $100.00 – 150.00.

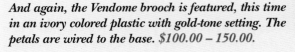

And again, the Vendome brooch is featured, this time in an ivory colored plastic with gold-tone setting. The petals are wired to the base. $100.00 – 150.00.

Massive acetate flower with matching earrings is accented with amethyst and pink rhinestones in a japanned setting. The brooch measures almost 4" in diameter and the earrings measure 1½". These sets by Vendome are highly collectible. Just the earrings are signed "Vendome©." $200.00 – 300.00.

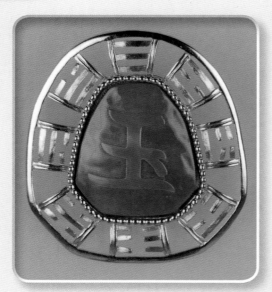

Pendant/brooch features a faux jade insert inscribed with the Chinese character for "graceful." It measures almost 2½ " wide and 2¾" long. Signed "Hattie©Carnegie" on an oval cartouche. $100.00 – 150.00.

The Hattie Carnegie pendant/brooch shown in a marbled coral color, this time with matching chain. $100.00 – 150.00.

Left: Asian-inspired faux jade pendant is very large and measures 3" in diameter. Signed "Vendome©." $125.00 – 175.00. Right: A Chinese junket features faux jade components. This brooch design was also made in faux coral and ivory. It measures 2¼" x 2¼" and is signed "Hattie©Carnegie" on an oval cartouche. $200.00 – 250.00.

Same design as previous brooch, this time featured in faux ivory. Signed "Vendome©." $125.00 – 175.00.

This magnificent molded plastic brooch from Boucher features the serene countenance of an Asian princess; the ornate headdress and necklace are lined with crystal clear rhinestones; gold-plated setting. Signed "BOUCHER©." A design number is included. The brooch measures 2¼" wide x 2½" tall. $300.00 – 400.00.

Hattie Carnegie smiling clown face features faux jade face with pearl nose, crystal clear rhinestone trim, and enameled accents. Brooch measures 2½" tall, signed "Hattie©Carnegie." $250.00 – 300.00.

Large and heavy Vendome lion brooch features a swirl of faux ivory topped with enameled collar. Signed "Vendome©." $150.00 – 200.00.

Serene swan features a faux turquoise body with enameled accents and beautiful amethyst colored rhinestones. The neck and head are made from faux ivory colored plastic. This unsigned Hattie Carnegie brooch measures 2¼" tall. $200.00 – 300.00.

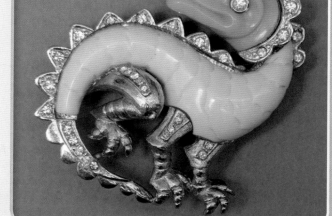

Fabulous dragon with faux ivory body and turquoise head is full of expression. The brooch measures 2" x 2" and is signed "KENNETH LANE" with no © symbol. $400.00 – 500.00.

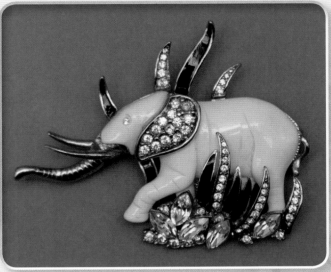

Left: Unsigned Pegasus pin is made with faux turquoise and coral plastic; the shiny gold-tone setting is made in one piece and accented with aurora borealis chatons. $50.00 – 75.00.
Right: Mythological Pegasus brooch by KRAMER© features faux jade and coral plastic inserts in a beautifully crafted pin. It measures 2" x 2"; the brushed gold-tone two-piece setting is trimmed with crystal clear rhinestones. $75.00 – 125.00.

Huge elephant brooch features ivory colored plastic inserts, enameled accents, and crystal clear rhinestones in the "grass." It measures 3" wide x 2½" high. Unsigned Hattie Carnegie. $300.00 – 400.00.

Brooch featuring a boy riding a dolphin is set in gold-plated metal and features faux jade, turquoise, and coral inserts. Made in two pieces, this large brooch measures 3" long. Unsigned Hattie Carnegie. $500.00 – 600.00.

King Neptune is riding the waves in this unsigned piece featuring faux jade, turquoise, and coral inserts. The substantial brooch is attributed to Hattie Carnegie and is made in two pieces. It measures 2¼" x 2¼". $500.00 – 600.00.

Faux ivory fish looks like he is leaping over the waves. Signed "SPINX," this piece measures 3" long. $150.00 – 200.00.

Four petitie turtles are featured in this photo; the plain shell turtle is signed "KJL©;" the others are signed "KENNETH LANE©." The studded turtles also have crystal clear rhinestone trim. All measure 1½" in length. $50.00 – 75.00 each.

Yellow plastic cabochon serves as the shell for this tortoise, set in gold tone with pavé set rhinestone trim. The brooch measures 2¼" long x 1½" wide. Signed "DeNicola©" on an oval cartouche. $75.00 – 100.00.

Majestic heron brooch measures 3"
tall and is unsigned, attributed to
Hattie Carnegie. $500.00 – 600.00.

*Different color scheme is
featured on this heron
brooch but otherwise it is
the same design and mea-
surements. Unsigned, attributed to Hattie Carnegie.
$500.00 – 600.00.*

*Brightly colored toucans feature a variety
of plastic inserts and enameled trim.
Each measures 3½" in length. Left bird is
unsigned; middle bird is signed "Kenneth
©Lane"; right brooch is signed "KJL©."
$100.00 – 125.00 each.*

You can't have too many toucans, that's my philosophy. Three more are featured in this photograph. Top center bird with coral colored beak is signed "Hattie Carnegie©"; the ivory beaked bird is unsigned; the bird with black beak and turquoise and coral inserts is signed "©KJL." $100.00 – 125.00 each.

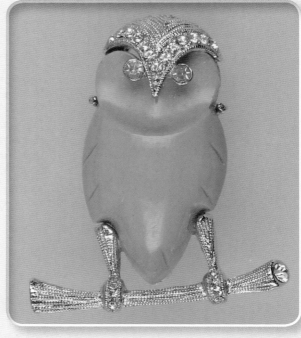

Pensive owl features a large coral colored plastic body and crystal clear rhinestone trim in a silver-tone setting. It measures 2½" tall. Signed "Hattie© Carnegie." $125.00 – 175.00.

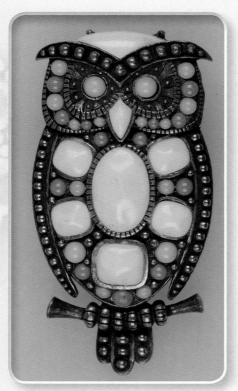

Massive owl brooch/pendant features faux turquoise, coral, and ivory plastic inserts. It measures 3¼" long. Unsigned. $75.00 – 100.00.

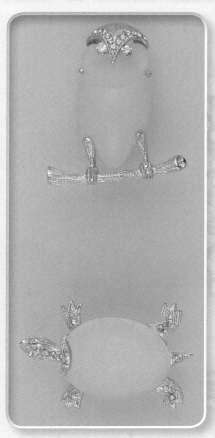

Frosted Lucite pieces from Hattie Carnegie include the owl and turtle brooches featured in this photo. Both are set in silver tone and have crystal clear rhinestone trim; each is signed "Hattie©Carnegie" on an oval cartouche. This series also featured a rooster design. $125.00 – 175.00 each.

Top: Hattie Carnegie butterfly brooch with wings that are mounted on springs so that they quiver with the wearer's movement. Signed "Hattie© Carnegie," this substantial brooch measures 3" at its widest point. $175.00 – 225.00.
Bottom: Moth brooch features molded faux jade wings, pavé set rhinestones, and peach enamel trim. Signed "©KJL," the brooch measures 3½" wide x 2" long. $125.00 – 175.00.

Imposing lion sits amid enameled grasses, some lined with clear rhinestones. His gold-plated mane encircles his molded faux turquoise face. Signed "Hattie©Carnegie," this colorful brooch measures 2½ " tall. $300.00 – 500.00.

Top: Faux ivory elephant brooch is so dimensional it can stand on its own. Signed "NETTIE ROSENSTEIN"; collectors prize the plastic pieces from Ms. Rosenstein. $300.00 – 400.00.
Bottom: Unsigned brooch/pendant is shown without its chain. This piece measures 3" long and 2½" high. Similar to a Hattie Carnegie design. $75.00 – 125.00.

Measuring an inch high, this dimensional deer can stand on its own; white cabochons decorate the coat of this lovely brooch by Kenneth Lane; signed "KJL" on an oval cartouche. $100.00 – 150.00.

Aztec warrior brooch by Kenneth Lane features a large faux turquoise cabochon and topaz stone set into the ornate gold-plated setting. This magnificent piece measures 3" tall x 2" wide and is signed "K.J.L." $400.00 – 600.00.

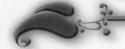
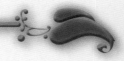

Plastic mask brooches in gold-plated metal are from Kenneth Lane. In his book entitled **Faking It,** *Mr. Lane says of his mask brooches, "Inca, Aztec, Mayan, take your pick. But the Verdura-inspired jade mask is definitely Olmec." Both the faux coral and black jade or onyx masks can be worn as pendants or brooches; both are signed "©KJL." The larger mask measures 2" x 2". $200.00 – 250.00.*
Smaller brooch measures 1½" x 1½". $175.00 – 225.00.
The Olmec civilization was pre-Columbian and situated in South Central Mexico. Olmec artwork is considered to be among the most striking and beautiful of the world's masterpieces. The civilization was most well known for its colossal head statues which were made of jade.

Happy Buddha pin is set in detailed gold tone. He measures 2¼" high and is unsigned. $100.00 – 150.00.

Larry Vrba designs and makes his own line of unique jewelry; only the highest quality components are used in these works of art. Although this piece is a brooch, it is massive and would certainly need to be worn on a coat or heavy jacket. The brooch measures 6" tall and 3½" wide. The centerpiece is a bearded faux ivory figure with a lamb nestled at his feet. Signed "LAWRENCE VRBA" on an oval cartouche. $400.00 – 500.00.
Right: Back of Vrba brooch showing the components and signature cartouche.

Smiling Asian figure, this piece, which is signed "ART©," could easily be mistaken for HAR. It measures 2½" tall x 1½" wide. $200.00 – 250.00.

Headhunter brooch from Kenneth Lane; this version features a pale green face with faux turquoise and coral accents. The headpiece is a row of faux pearls; this brooch measures 2" tall x 1¾" wide. Signed "KENNETH LANE©." $175.00 – 225.00.

Recognizable antelope brooch by Hattie Carnegie is always popular among collectors and for good reason. This well-made brooch features many details including faux coral horns and turquoise face in a gold-plated setting. Impressively sized at almost 4" long, this pieces is signed "Hattie©Carnegie" on an oval cartouche. $300.00 – 400.00.

Portly pig brooch is by Kenneth Lane. The design is based on a ceramic pig he purchased while in Venice; the original was destroyed in the mold making. This pin measures 2" long x 2" wide and features a resin pearl belly. Signed "KENNETH LANE©." $100.00 – 150.00.

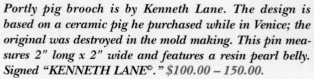

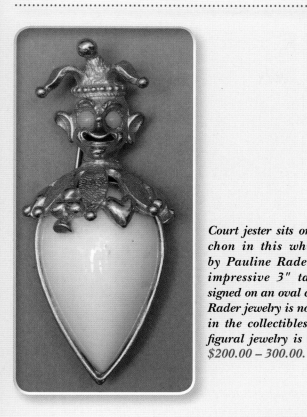

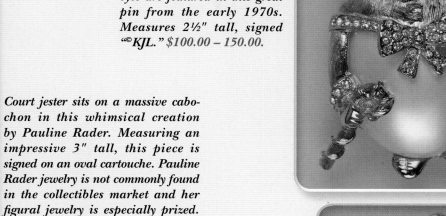

Pictured here with cane, top hat, and bowtie, perhaps Humpty Dumpty will rethink sitting on the wall? Resin pearl body, shiny gold and silver-tone finish, and emerald eyes are featured in this great pin from the early 1970s. Measures 2½" tall, signed "© KJL." $100.00 – 150.00.

Court jester sits on a massive cabochon in this whimsical creation by Pauline Rader. Measuring an impressive 3" tall, this piece is signed on an oval cartouche. Pauline Rader jewelry is not commonly found in the collectibles market and her figural jewelry is especially prized. $200.00 – 300.00.

Unsigned Hattie Carnegie brooch features a reclining mermaid resting on her faux jade shell. Measuring 2¾" long, this brooch is made in two pieces and riveted together. $200.00 – 300.00.

Unsigned Kenneth Lane brooches date from the 1960s. These magnificent pieces are signed "KJL Laguna©."
Left: suspended in the ocean's depths, the Queen plays her instrument for the King. $400.00 – 600.00.
Right: King Neptune, who measures an imposing 3" in length, blows his horn. $400.00 – 600.00.

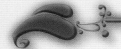

Perky fish features white molded plastic inserts. It measures 2" long x 2½" from top to bottom. Signed "MONET©." $35.00 – 50.00.

Boucher brooch features faux jade "scales" set into shiny gold tone. Signed "BOUCHER©" with a design number, this piece measures 3" tall x 2" wide. $50.00 – 75.00.

Beautiful plastic flower brooch by Jomaz is accented with a golden bee whose wings are trimmed with crystal clear rhinestones. Signed "JOMAZ©." $200.00 – 250.00.

Lovely lily of the valley is featured in this floral brooch, signed "KRAMER©." Enameled accents and aurora borealis chatons add pretty details to this demure brooch. It measures 2½" tall x 1½" wide. $100.00 – 150.00.

Hattie Carnegie's take on the spring lily of the valley is shown in this brooch that measures 3" tall x 1¼" wide. Signed "Hattie©Carnegie." $100.00 – 150.00.

Pearlescent cups are featured on yet another version of the beloved lily of the valley, this time tied together in a bouquet. Signed "KJL©," the brooch measures 3" tall x 1¾" wide. $75.00 – 125.00.

From Sarah Coventry, this leaf brooch is named "Autumn Splendor." It is made with coral colored plastic and set in gold tone. Signed "SARAHCOV©." $35.00 – 60.00.

Maltese cross features crystal clear rhinestones and turquoise pear shaped cabochons. Signed "K.J.L.," it measures 3½" in diameter. $300.00 – 400.00.

A striking color combination is featured in this newer Kenneth Lane Maltese cross which can be worn as a pendant or brooch. It measures 3½" wide and is signed "©KJL" and "CHINA." $75.00 – 125.00.

Faux jade spikes adorn this magnificent brooch from TRIFARI©. It measures 2½" x 2½" and is set in sturdy gold-plated metal. $75.00 – 125.00.

The Art Deco influence can be seen in this massive brooch/pendant from Kenneth Lane. It measures 3" x 3"; the faux jade centerpiece is set off beautifully with the black enameled accents. Signed "KENNETH LANE©." $100.00 – 150.00.

Age of Aquarius

The Age of Aquarius was a popular theme for costume jewelry in the 1960s. It was captured beautifully by two companies in particular, including Luke Razza and Jerry DeNicola.

Sign	Symbol	Dates
Aries	Ram	3/21 – 4/19
Taurus	Bull	4/20 – 5/20
Gemini	Twins	5/21 – 6/20
Cancer	Crab	6/21 – 7/22
Leo	Lion	7/23 – 8/22
Virgo	Virgin	8/23 – 9/22
Libra	Balance	9/23 – 10/22
Scorpio	Scorpion	10/23 – 11/21
Sagittarius	Archer	11/22 – 12/21
Capricorn	Goat	12/22 – 1/19
Aquarius	Water Bearer	1/20 – 2/18
Pisces	Fish	2/19 – 3/20

Virgo the virgin is depicted in this massive faux ivory pendant which measures almost 4" long; signed "RAZZA©." $100.00 – 150.00.

Taurus the bull is depicted in this detailed and dimensional pendant and ring by RAZZA©. Both pieces are signed; pendant, $75.00 – 125.00; ring, $35.00 – 60.00.

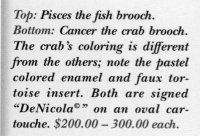

Top center: Leo the lion is depicted and is signed "DeNicola©" on an oval cartouche. The friendly feline holds a star set with clear rhinestones.

Following clockwise: Aquarius the water bearer is depicted next; the Gemini twins can be worn as a brooch or necklace; and Virgo the virgin is on the left. These lovely pieces feature colorful enameling, crystal clear rhinestones, and faux coral, turquoise, and jade inserts. All are signed "DeNicola©" on an oval cartouche. $200.00 – 300.00 each.

Top: Pisces the fish brooch.
Bottom: Cancer the crab brooch. The crab's coloring is different from the others; note the pastel colored enamel and faux tortoise insert. Both are signed "DeNicola©" on an oval cartouche. $200.00 – 300.00 each.

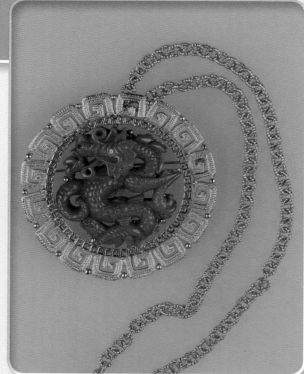

The Asian influence can be seen in this massive brooch/pendant from Hattie Carnegie. The beautifully rendered dragon is very dimensional; the piece measures 3" in diameter. $300.00 – 400.00.

Florenza necklace shows the Asian influence in this faux jade pendant with antiqued gold-tone setting. This large piece measures 3" wide x 3½" long. Signed "FLORENZA©." $75.00 – 125.00.

Unsigned Hattie Carnegie piece features faux ivory with enameled accents. This piece can be worn as a brooch or pendant; it measures 2½" across x 5" (including chains). $150.00 – 200.00.

Faux jade pieces by Vendome feature a pendant and matching earrings. Pendant measures 3¾" long x 2½" wide; the chain is attached on each side of the pendant and each length measures 16". The earrings measure 2¼" long. The brooch is similar but not part of the set. It measures 3" x 2¼". All pieces are signed "Vendome©." Pendant and earrings, $150.00 – 200.00; brooch, $125.00 – 175.00.

Sea Swirl pendant from Avon measures 2" long x 1" wide. Lightweight due to the plastic material from which it is made, it is signed "AVON" on a metal hang tag. $25.00 – 40.00.

Exquisite Avon necklace features a large pear shaped pink cabochon. This piece dates to 1974 and was named "Pale Fire." It measures 2¼ " long and has sparkling clear rhinestones around the perimeter of the pendant. Signed "AVON©." $35.00 – 50.00.

Stylized elephant pendant measures 2" x 2". Set in shiny gold tone. Unsigned. $35.00 – 50.00.

This faux blue lapis choker-length necklace features molded plastic inserts set in shiny gold tone. Signed "KENNETH LANE" on a small cartouche near the clasp. $75.00 – 125.00.

This large, bib-style Goldette necklace has faux turquoise accents, circa 1960s. Chain measures 20" long; the pendant almost 5". Signed "Goldette." $100.00 – 150.00.

Left: Convertible Kenneth Jay Lane bolo-style necklace can be transformed by removing this pendant and replacing it with the large resin pearl pendant for a completely different look. Each snaps on and off. Signed "KJL©." $50.00 – 75.00. Right: Detail of resin pearl pendant from KJL necklace.

"*Jeweltone Statement Necklace*" *is the name of this piece. The centerpiece is huge and measures 5½" wide x 3" deep. Signed "KJL." $125.00 – 175.00.*

In the early 1970s Les Bernard introduced a line of necklaces made of real Baltic amber. The line was part of a larger collection of jewelry made from jade, horn, coral, and mother-of-pearl. This amber necklace is from that line and is signed with a hang tag. $100.00 – 150.00.

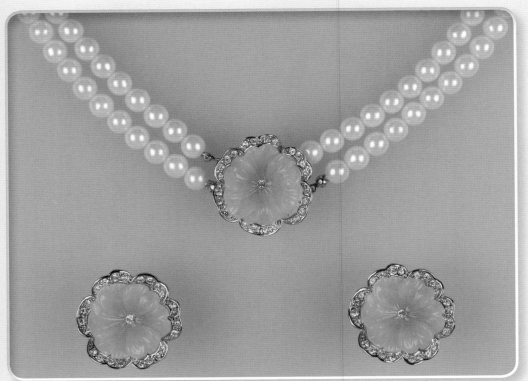

Ram's head necklace is by Kenneth Lane for Avon. It measures 32" long and features plastic onyx beads, subtle crystal clear rhinestone trim, and green rhinestone eyes. Signed "K.J.L. for Avon." This was part of a set that features a gold-tone clamper bracelet and matching earrings (not shown). Necklace, $50.00 – 100.00.

"Perfect Pansy" set from Avon features a double strand of pearls finished with pink plastic pansies. The necklace measures 20" long; clip earrings are 1¼" in diameter. All pieces are signed "K.J.L. for Avon." $125.00 – 175.00.

Kenneth Jay Lane necklace and matching earrings date to 1993. From the Avon "Caprianti" collection, the set features massive plastic cabochons. To give you some idea of the scale of this piece, the cabochons each measure from 1½" to 2" wide. Signed "K.J.L. for AVON." $125.00 – 175.00 set.

Black plastic beads contrast beautifully with the molded white plastic rose in this lovely early 1990s set from Avon. The set was also made with white beads and a black center rose; rosebud earrings match the centerpiece. All pieces are signed "K.J.L. for Avon." $125.00 – 175.00 set.

"Midnight Rose" set by Kenneth Lane for Avon. $125.00 – 175.00.

This summery set from Mimi di Niscemi is dated 1973. Triple-strand necklace features tiny yellow spacers that pick up the enameled daisy centerpiece. Matching daisy earrings complete the ensemble and are signed twice, "Mimi di N." $150.00 – 200.00.

Pendant-style necklace features massive black onyx cabochon which itself measures almost 2" long and 1" deep. With the dangle, the pendant measures just over 3" long. The 24" chain features crystal clear prong set rhinestones; fish hook clasp. Unsigned beauty. $50.00 – 75.00.

Lovely fish pendant on 24" chain features plastic fins encased in gold which move with the wearer's movement. The pendant is 3¾" long x 1½" wide. Unsigned. $35.00 – 50.00.

Givenchy Bakelite perfume bottle is featured; the chain necklace measures 28"; the pendant is 2" tall. The tiny metal hang tag provides a wealth of information including the year (1978); signed "©GIVENCHY Paris-New York." $150.00 – 200.00.

Faux tortoise maple leaf necklace and matching earrings date from the 1970s and are signed "TRIFARI©." Gold-tone snake chain is marked with a hang tag and measures 20" long. $50.00 – 100.00 set.

From the 1970s, a solid perfume pendant from Max Factor is of the scent named "Khara." The pendant measures 2¼" in diameter; the chain measures 27" long. To gain access to the intact perfume, the gold-tone piece on the back flips up and voilá! The scent was recently retired by the company. $50.00 – 75.00.

In the early 1970s Butler and Wilson designed a line of Pierrot bracelets, brooches, and necklaces in plastic. The bracelets were etched and painted Galalith; they sometimes included rhinestone accents. These bangles are from that line. Unsigned, $200.00 – 300.00 each.

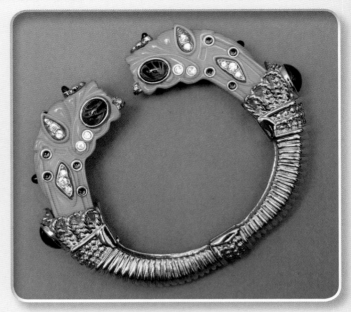

Magnificent sea serpent clamper from PAULINE RADER features large blue lapis and faux turquoise cabochons in a gold-plated bracelet. Note the "scales" and fin details. Signed on an oval cartouche. $400.00 – 600.00.

Fabulous Cartier-inspired bangle from Kenneth Jay Lane features faux coral dragon heads with green cabochon accents. The bangle features a unique spring clasp that keeps it both tight and comfortable on the wrist. $400.00 – 600.00.

Vendome quality is on full view in this triple-strand memory bracelet and matching earrings in brushed gold tone. The beads are red plastic; the matching earrings measure 2½" long; both pieces feature rondelles with prong set rhinestones. Just the clip-back earrings are signed "Vendome." $100.00 – 150.00.

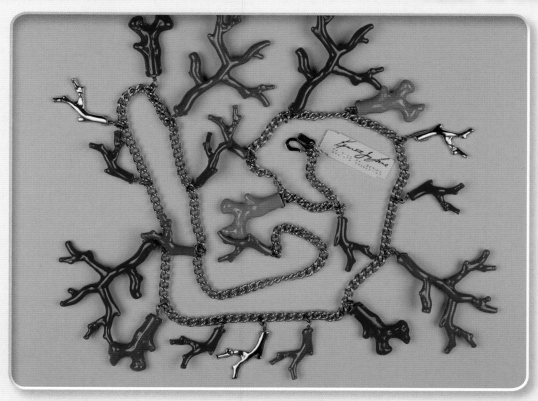

From the Kenneth Jay Lane couture collection comes this early 1970s belt featuring large and small pieces of faux branch coral. The larger pieces of coral measure over 3" long! When purchased, the belt cost $375.00. Marked with a metal hang tag, "©KENNETH LANE." Price today, $600.00 – 800.00.

Hattie Carnegie ram's head earrings were made to coordinate with other pieces including a highly collectible clamper bracelet. Signed "Hattie©Carnegie." $100.00 – 150.00.

Wooden Jewelry

Carved wood was a favorite material for costume jewelry during the 1930s and 1940s. While Western and Mexican motifs are among the most popular subjects there were many others as well. One that appeared again and again was the Scottie dog. Certainly President Franklin D. Roosevelt's Scottie, Fala, was the most famous dog in the world during the early 1940s. By all accounts, FDR and Fala were inseparable. From negotiations with heads of state to delivering the regular radio address, Fala was by the side of the President.

From the 1930s to the 1950s home craft kits were used to make jewelry. Instructions could be found in books about whittling and carving, as well as in popular hobby and fashion magazines. Hobbyists were encouraged to carve a beloved pet in wood, and directions were included on how to fasten the pin back to the brooch. Several costume jewelry designers and manufacturers also sold jewelry made with wood and wood accents, including Miriam Haskell, Coro, Elzac, Castlecliff, Chanel, and Schiaparelli. Other companies who produced wood and wood/plastic combination jewelry are Alta Novelty Company, Ace Plastic, California Craft Company, Authentics, Inc. Hobby House, and California Treasures. Signatures are almost nonexistent on most jewelry made wholly from wood. The exception is the home craftsman who sometimes signed his pieces.

This cowgirl measures over 4" tall. Details include fringe accent on her jodhpurs. This large lady measures 4½" tall. $100.00 – 150.00.

Leather and paint details, combined with the plastic cigarette, add interest to this cowpoke and increase his value to collectors. Brooch measures 4" x 2¼". $175.00 – 225.00.

Prepare to be serenaded by this musician whose arm moves with the wearer's movement. The brooch measures 3¾" x 1½" at widest. Paint details show very little wear. $150.00 – 200.00.

Simple stamped brooch features paint details. It measures 2¾" high. $35.00 – 50.00.

Chinese water carrier is a figure that is seldom seen in wood, but frequently appears in cast pieces. It measures almost 4" tall; with paint details, $175.00 – 225.00.

Dutch boy with painted wood and cheerful expression measures 4½ " high. $50.00 – 75.00.

Lots of detail in this scarecrow brooch, including plastic shoes, hands, and cap as well as raffia at the neck. This large brooch (measures 4¼") is in excellent condition, adding to its value. $200.00 – 300.00 and up.

This figural brooch is an example of jewelry made from a kit. The backing is a perforated metal and the beads are strung on wire. Figure is 4½" tall. $35.00 – 50.00.

This is a huge brooch, made in one piece with accents that include paint details, glass eye for the horse, and leather accents on the rider. It measures 4" tall x 3" wide. $175.00 – 225.00.

This cowboy was carved in a separate piece and fastened to the horse with a metal rivet. A very dimensional piece in excellent condition, this large brooch measures 4" tall x almost 4" wide. $175.00 – 225.00.

Alta Novelty Company produced wooden jewelry accented with Bakelite from about 1935 – 1940. This piece is in immaculate condition, measures 4" tall, and features wood, metal, fabric, and a Bakelite monkey. $225.00 – 300.00.

Another combination piece that features wood with Bakelite accents. Measuring almost 4" tall, this bear is carrying a pail made of Bakelite. His arm moves with the wearer's movement. Paint accents add detail. $225.00 – 300.00.

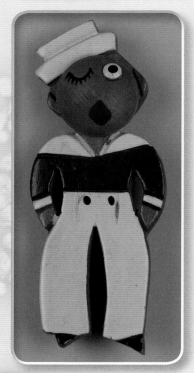

Sailor brooch features paint details and is in excellent condition. The face is glued onto the figure. $75.00 – 125.00.

Sailor brooch features paint details and moveable legs. The face on this figure is also applied. It measures 3" tall. $75.00 – 125.00.

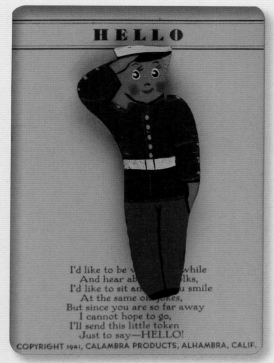

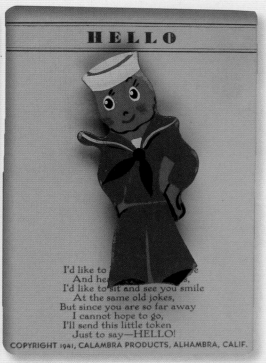

Left: World War II brooch marked "Copyright 1941, Calambra Products, Alhambra, Calif." It measures 3" tall, is made from lightweight wood, and has overall painting. $25.00 – 50.00.
Right: This pin was also made by Calambra Products. The poem on each card reads, "I'd like to be with you awhile And hear about the folks, I'd like to sit and see you smile At the same old jokes, But since you are so far away, I cannot hope to go, I'll send this little token Just to say HELLO!" $25.00 – 50.00.

*Left: Striding Uncle Sam measures 2½"
tall. $75.00 – 125.00.
Right: Sailor, which measures 2¼", is
actually a fur clip. $50.00 – 100.00.*

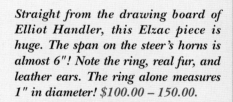

*Straight from the drawing board of
Elliot Handler, this Elzac piece is
huge. The span on the steer's horns is
almost 6"! Note the ring, real fur, and
leather ears. The ring alone measures
1" in diameter! $100.00 – 150.00.*

*Horse pins made from wood are readily available in the
collectibles market and the variations are interesting and
fun to collect. The Lucite on this Elzac piece is dimensional and fluid; the carved wood face with paint details
sits on top of the Lucite; the pieces are glued together.
Brooch measures 2½" x 3" wide. $125.00 – 175.00.*

Lucite mane is attached with rivets; painted teeth and eye add interest to this horse brooch. It measures 2½" tall x almost 3" wide. $50.00 – $75.00.

Carved horse head has glass eye and metal and plastic accents, and measures 3" high x 2½" wide. Metal clasp is attached with rivets. $75.00 – 100.00.

Equestrian brooch features a horse head carved from a darker wood than the base of the brooch, providing contrast. The head is attached with a screw. The leather square is laced onto the wood with plastic; the same plastic is featured in the reins. The brooch measures 3½" wide x 1½" deep. $75.00 – 125.00.

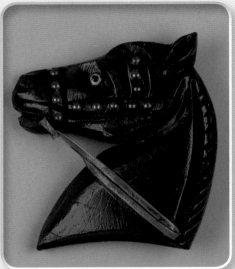

This massive brooch measures 4 inches tall by 2½" wide. Details include a glass eye, metal bit, and plastic reins. The carving is particularly detailed on this piece. $75.00 – 100.00.

The eye is painted on in this character that measures 3" tall. $35.00 – 50.00.

This brooch appears to have a coat of lacquer or varnish which has kept it shiny for many years. It features a glass eye, brass studs, and leather reins. Heavily carved, the pin measures 2½" x 2¼". $75.00 – 100.00.

Horse racing was a favorite pastime in the 1940s and 1950s. These three are obviously in a race to the finish. They are heavily carved with plastic reins and measure 3½" wide. Eyes are painted on. $75.00 – 100.00.

The three horses above seem to be trying hard to win in a race to the finish line; each has a glass eye, painted accents, and plastic reins. Beautifully carved, $100.00 – 125.00. Is it the victor in the photo on the right? Lucky horse brooch measures 2½" wide x 2¾" tall; painted accents, $75.00 – 100.00.

Heavily carved and dimensional horses adorn this clamper-style bracelet. Rare and very collectible. $200.00 – 300.00.

Beautiful horse with finely carved mane, plastic reins, and painted eye measures almost 4" tall. $75.00 – 100.00.

Painted sombreros adorn this nicely carved fellow with painted details and glass eye. The strings have lost some of their plastic coating, not uncommon in these pieces. $75.00 – 100.00.

A horse needs a saddle, and a rider needs boots, and here they are. Leather detail on saddle is affixed with metal studs. Brooch measures 3" wide x 2" tall; paint details are in excellent shape. $125.00 – 150.00.

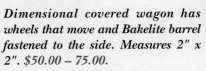

Dimensional covered wagon has wheels that move and Bakelite barrel fastened to the side. Measures 2" x 2". $50.00 – 75.00.

Scottie dogs showed up as often as did horses, and were found in both wood and Bakelite. This beautifully carved piece has a metal and plastic collar and a painted eye. It measures 2½" x 2½". $50.00 – 75.00.

This detailed piece of furniture actually has metal drawer pulls. It measures 2" tall x 1¼" wide. $50.00 – 75.00.

Lightweight pin with bar signed "Midge" features a hanging dog. $20.00 – 35.00.

Cute pup pin has a rear end which can move; a bit of pipe cleaner serves as the tail. This piece is lightly signed "Betty" in pencil on the back and measures 2½" x 2½". $25.00 – 40.00.

Popular Scottie dog is heavily carved. It measures 2¾" x 2¾" and features a simple c-clasp. $50.00 – 75.00.

Pair of dogs are featured in a light colored wood with lots of carving. With painted eyes and roll-over clasp, the brooch measures 2¼" wide x 2" high. $35.00 – 50.00.

This is a very dimensional and heavily carved piece which measures 3" tall x 2¾" at widest. The wood seems to shimmer. $50.00 – 75.00.

Very large Scottie pin measures 3" tall x 2½" wide. Painted details include the eyes and tongue; heavy carving gives the appearance of hair. $50.00 – 75.00.

Painted wood brooch is smaller than most, measuring just 1½" x 1½". I believe this may be a piece that was carved by a hobbyist, perhaps a rendering of a favorite pet. It is a delicate and beautiful piece. $25.00 – 40.00.

At first I thought this piece was plastic made to look like wood. But it is made of a slice of very hard wood with painted accent and measures just 1½" x 1½". Curiously, it is signed with the initials "JCC."
$25.00 – 40.00.

Like a piece of fine sculpture, you can see the carver's marks in this dimensional piece. Leather collar, glass eye, and a smattering of paint accents complete this piece that measures 3" tall x 2¾" wide. $75.00 – 100.00.

This brooch is simply carved with paint accents and a simple C-clasp. It measures 2¼" x 2¼". $25.00 – 40.00.

Simpler yet, this piece is actually a dress clip. It measures 1¾" high x 1½" at its widest. $15.00 – 25.00.

Could this be a playful Pinocchio before he realized he was a donkey? Measuring 2½" x 2½", this piece features paint details. $35.00 – 50.00.

Elephant features some carving and paint details. Large ears are perhaps not as large as Dumbo's, but that's who this whimsical figure reminds me of. This large piece measures 3" wide x 2½" at its tallest. $35.00 – 50.00.

The wood grain is used to advantage in this beautifully carved giraffe. This large brooch measures 4" tall and features a glass eye and minimal painted accents. $100.00 – 125.00.

This happy bear with googly eye is a fun piece that measures 2¼" x 1¾". $25.00 – 50.00.

This kitty has a painted design with shellac finish and measures almost 3" tall x 2" wide. This type of wooden jewelry is fairly common in the collectibles market and is of less interest to collectors than pieces which feature heavy carving and various accents. $15.00 – 30.00.

This lightweight wooden brooch features a head mounted on a spring so it bounces around with the wearer's movements. This is a large version of a fairly common type of pin and measures 3" tall x 2½" wide. It is stamped "JAPAN." $25.00 – 40.00.

These lightweight wooden brooches feature heads mounted on springs. These smaller versions are more commonly found in the collectibles market and measure just 1" wide x 1¾" tall. With painted accents, these are stamped "JAPAN." $15.00 – 25.00.

A mixed media piece, this turtle brooch has a wooden base and a Bakelite shell. A large and beautiful piece which measures almost 3" long, these are valued by collectors. $300.00 – 400.00.

This majestic Elzac piece was featured in the "Jewels of Fantasy" exhibit and shown in the accompanying catalog. Metal studs and carved Lucite horns provide details which are coveted by collectors. This piece was made from ebony. Elzac brooches were marked with hang tags which were removed before wearing. To find a piece with the hang tag intact is a collector's dream. It measures 4" tall x 3½" at its widest. $200.00 – 300.00.

Petite duck pin measures just 1½" x 1½". The paint accents are in excellent condition. $25.00 – 40.00.

Left: Whimsical duck features a glass eye and painted accents, heavily carved. The pin measures 3" tall. $50.00 – 75.00.
Right: Beautiful details abound on this huge parrot brooch measuring 4" long. It features a glass eye and paint details with some wear to the paint. $75.00 – 100.00.

A plastic body and separate plastic head are affixed to the wooden base in this beautiful bird pin with painted accents. The delicate brooch is in excellent condition and measures 3" x 3". $100.00 – 150.00.

This whimsical duck with a happy expression is what makes these brooches so much fun to collect. The wood cap is separate and fastened with a rivet; leather and paint accents are in great shape. $75.00 – 125.00.

Graceful stork with molded plastic legs looks like he might have misplaced the baby. This hefty fellow measures 3½" tall x 4" wide. $100.00 – 150.00.

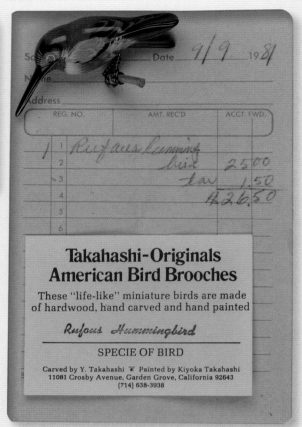

Top: Fortunate collectors have no problem identifying this pin made by the Takahashis. It came with paperwork and receipt; it is also signed with the initials "K.T." for the artist, Kiyoka Takahashi. In the event you find one with no markings or paperwork, look for pin backs that were affixed with push-in nails. $200.00 – 300.00 and up. Right: original paperwork with Takahashi brooch, including receipt.

Takahashi-Originals American Bird Brooches

These "life-like" miniature birds are made of hardwood, hand carved and hand painted

Rufous Hummingbird

SPECIE OF BIRD

Carved by Y. Takahashi ❦ Painted by Kiyoka Takahashi
11081 Crosby Avenue, Garden Grove, California 92643
(714) 638-3938

Gorgeous Takahashi golden pheasant brooch has the characteristic push-in pin back. Inspiration for the vibrant and colorful Takahashi pheasants came from the National Association of Audubon Society publications. This large brooch measures almost 4" in length. Unsigned. $300.00 – 400.00 and up.

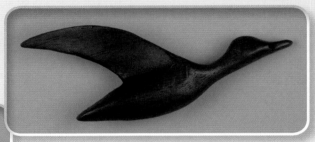

Graceful duck features a simple but dimensional design. This is a more contemporary piece, probably 1970s. $15.00 – 30.00.

Unusual wooden chatelaine features mom and baby chipmunks. Mom is 1¾" tall; baby is 1" tall. $35.00 – 50.00.

These unusual squirrel earrings have plastic screw-back components. $15.00 – 25.00.

Massive monkey sports a felt cap attached with a plastic strap. Beautifully carved and well preserved paint details increase the value of this Elzac piece. It measures 3½" x 3½". $125.00 – 150.00.

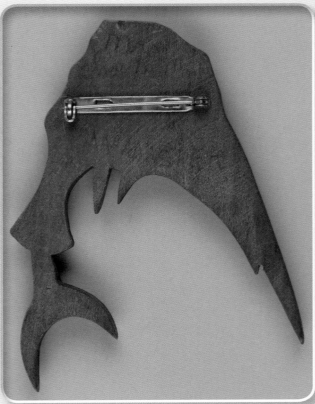

Left: Swordfish brooches were common during the 1940s and were made in many materials including metal, plastic, plastic and wood combinations, and of course, just wood. This is a heavily carved piece with painted eye and measures 2½" wide x 3". $75.00 – 100.00.
Right: Back of the swordfish brooch shows a pencil signature that reads "Mrs Chas McMaster."

This combination brooch from Elzac features a glass eye and Lucite fins which are made in one large piece and fastened with a rivet. A graceful piece. $100.00 – 150.00.

Carved and painted black, this large female face features rhinestone accents and measures 2¾" wide x 3½" tall. The bow in her hair is a separate piece of wood affixed with a metal screw. $100.00 – 150.00.

Apache dancer pin features lots of detail including a fabric scarf, metal earring with plastic bead, painted cap, and plastic cigarette. He measures 3¼" tall x 2¾" wide. $150.00 – 200.00.

Carved and painted World War I sailor brooch with paint intact except for the U.S.A. on his cap. Features painted cigarette, plastic nose, and googly eyes. He measures 3" tall. $100.00 – 150.00.

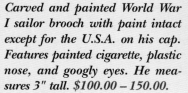

Native head pin measures 2¾" tall and features metal accents with geometric carving reminiscent of an African mask. $75.00 – 100.00.

Ubangi native head pin with rope collar, rope hair accent, and metal earring. The paint is in great shape on this huge brooch, which measures 4" tall. $100.00 – 150.00.

Elzac sculptural native head pin features deep carving with metal accents. $100.00 – 125.00.

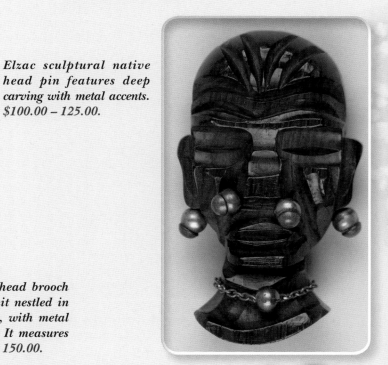

This Elzac native head brooch features plastic fruit nestled in the rope headdress, with metal and paint accents. It measures 4½" tall. $125.00 – 150.00.

Details abound in this heavily carved Elzac native head brooch with metal and plastic trim and a "grass" headdress. The brooch measures 4" tall. $125.00 – 150.00.

Elzac native pin with exaggerated features and paint trim which is completely intact. It measures 3" tall. $100.00 – 125.00.

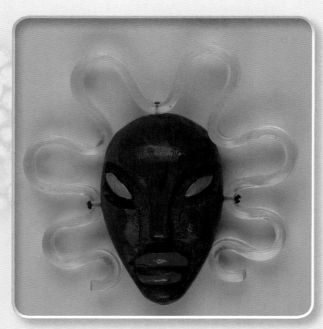

Beautiful Elzac design with curved Lucite trim and paint accents measures 3½" x 3½". The Lucite trim is affixed with metal screws. $150.00 – 200.00.

Another beautiful Elzac design with both Lucite and leather trim and some paint accents. This brooch measures 2½" wide x 3" tall. $150.00 – 200.00.

This is a marvelous example of wooden face jewelry with painted accents and plastic earrings. This beauty measures 4" tall. $200.00 – 225.00.

Laughing Eskimo face has fake fur trim, painted accents, and exaggerated features. This is a relatively small piece and measures just 1½" x 1½". $50.00 – 75.00.

This brooch has beautiful detail including the headdress and metal earrings. While some paint loss is noted, the value is largely unaffected because of the additional details. $175.00 – 225.00.

Native American face with detailed carving, no accents. It measures 3" tall x 2½" wide. The surface of the wood seems to shimmer. $75.00 – 100.00.

Wooden brooch features reverse-carved Lucite headdress and paint accents. The headdress is affixed to the wood using metal rivets. $100.00 – 150.00.

This heavily carved and painted piece with Egyptian motif measures a full 1¼" deep and 2¼" high. At its widest point it measures almost 2". $75.00 – 125.00.

Carved and paint details embellish this collectible Totem pole brooch, which measures almost 4" tall. $150.00 – 200.00.

This darling brooch was probably handmade at home; it features a real pecan, fabric head cover, and metal earrings. $25.00 – 40.00.

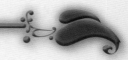

Beautiful celluloid cameo is mounted on three dif-ferent colors of wood slices which are glued together. Note the metal accents on the headdress and necklace. This measures 1½" tall x 1" wide. $25.00 – 40.00.

Wood and double laminated Bakelite brooch features a prong-set cameo. This measures 2½" wide x 2" tall. $150.00 – 200.00.

Carved celluloid is mounted on wood to fashion a femi-nine brooch. $25.00 – 40.00.

Real nuts are teamed with this carved wooden bar pin and carved leaves. The bar measures 3" wide x 2½" long, including dangling fruit. $75.00 – 125.00.

This do-it-yourself brooch is made with wooden balls and a slice of a real nut. Leather trim. $25.00 – 40.00.

Elzac design features carved wooden flowers with Lucite accents. The design, which measures 3" tall x 2½" wide, is based on an Elliot Handler design which was not patented. $100.00 – 150.00.

Big wooden button with intricate carved detail features the ubiquitous Scottie dog theme from the 1940s. It measures 1½" in diameter. $15.00 – 25.00.

Fabulous carved dress clips feature metal embellishments. It is unusual to find a pair; singles are much more common. The clip is stamped with a utility patent number, 1852188, granted to Elisha A. Phinney (designer) on 9/20/1932 for "brooch or clasp with an ornamental design." $125.00 – 175.00.

Every now and then an old shoe turns up. This whimsical brooch features plastic laces and measures 2" x 2". $25.00 – 40.00.

Ever-popular Mexican-themed necklace features painted sombrero, wooden balls, and celluloid chain. $50.00 – 75.00.

Real nuts embellish this celluloid chain. This unusual piece is in perfect condition. $75.00 – 100.00.

Carved leaves and nuts hang from
a shiny brass chain in this pretty
demi parure. $100.00 – 150.00.

Carved and stained wooden
beads are attached to a brass
chain in this necklace. Small
wood cubes accent each bead.
Czech. $175.00 – 225.00.

Marvelous Czech necklace features small wooden cubes strung together to make balls; dangling Galalith discs have celluloid ring accents. Celluloid and metal chain. Very lightweight, unsigned. $200.00 – 250.00.

Mid-century necklace and matching earrings feature alternating dark and light wood acorns. Unsigned. $75.00 – 100.00.

Memory bracelet, clip ear-rings, and necklace com-prise this parure made of smooth wooden beads. An unusual set. $75.00 – 125.00.

This bracelet features painted wooden beads made to look like fruit including bananas, apples, pears, oranges, and plums. The fruit is large, with each piece measuring ½". The chain is brass and the bracelet is probably Czech. $50.00 – 75.00.

Clamper-style bracelet features lots of carved accents including a graceful hand; note the metal bracelet adorning the wrist. The paint accents are showing plenty of wear, thus affecting the price. $100.00 – 150.00.

Light and dark wood discs alternate in this pretty link bracelet. $25.00 – 40.00.

Miriam Haskell bracelet and dress clip are unsigned Frank Hess designs from the 1940s. The silk-wrapped cord bracelet and coiled cord dress clip feature carved green wood beads, large tear-shaped wooden beads, and little star-shaped wooden beads in green, red, blue, yellow, and brown. The bracelet has a button closure and the dress clip has the perforated plastic back. The bracelet measures 7½" x 2½" while the dress clip measures 3⅛" x 2". $400.00 – 600.00.

Unsigned WWII Haskell dress clip features small dyed wood beads in a variety of colors; the leaves are pressed glass. The clip has a perforated plastic back. $250.00 – 350.00.

Cheerful and colorful Czech brooch features wooden beads, wired to a metal backing. It measures 2" in diameter and is marked "Czechoslovakia." $75.00 – 100.00.

The 1970s are back in this huge Maltese cross brooch/pendant. $35.00 – 50.00.

1930s purse with handles features colorful painted and stained wooden beads and zipper closing. It has a label on the inside which reads "Genuine Fast Color Wood Beads" and "Made in Czechoslovakia." It measures 6½" deep x 8½" wide. $125.00 – 150.00.

1930s purse with handles features colorful painted and stained wooden beads and zipper closing. It is signed on an inside label, "Suzanne" brand and "Made in Czechoslovakia." This purse measures 12½" wide x 5½" deep. $125.00 – 150.00.

The 1940s in Gold and Silver

Costume jewelry made during the 1940s features a variety of themes including striking geometric designs with bows, ribbons, and flowers that look like giant corsages. Often referred to as Retro modern, the brooches were massive and rhinestones were used sparingly. Sterling silver settings were often gold plated with rose and yellow gold. Shortages that resulted from rationing during WWII did not relent immediately after the war. Life returned to normal slowly and the shortages continued to be reflected in costume jewelry designs after 1945. Since many designs were patented during this time, it is often possible to locate the design patents which provide valuable historic records for collectors.

Magnificent Marcel Boucher TORII gate is signed with the Phrygian cap; it features enamel accented with crystal clear rhinestones. This gorgeous brooch measures 3¼" tall x 2½" wide. $800.00 – 1,000.00.

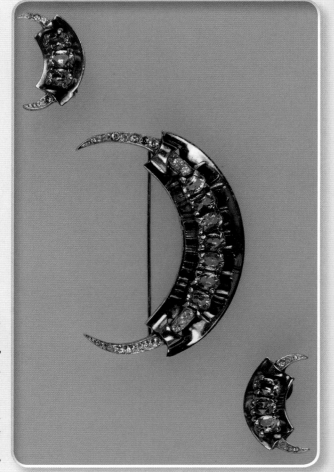

Striking design elements are featured in this demi parure by REJA. The earrings are signed twice, including on the clip mechanism, "STERLING SILVER" and "PAT PEND." The brooch is marked "STERLING" and measures 2½" tall. $150.00 – 200.00.
Before October 30, 1940 Reja was known as Deja. On this date, the New York Supreme Court issued an injunction restraining Deja Costume Jewelry from using "that name or any name similar to DUJAY, Inc. in connection with the manufacture or sale of novelty costume jewelry."

A popular design during the 1940s, this chatelaine-style brooch is signed "Coro" with the Pegasus symbol on a raised rectangle. When extended, the chain measures almost 7" long. $125.00 – 175.00.

Chatelaine-style brooch features Scottie dogs with rhinestone trim. A small flower at the fence post has a clear rhinestone. Chain measures 6" when extended. Unsigned. $100.00 – 150.00.

Two classic Retro Modern design brooches.
Upper right: Measures 3" at its widest; the stone alone measures almost an inch long. It is signed "CINER©." $150.00 – 200.00.
Lower left: This beautiful piece is marked "STERLING." Note the curlicue metal design. $150.00 – 200.00.

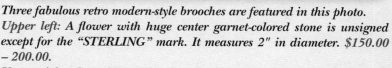

Three fabulous retro modern-style brooches are featured in this photo.
Upper left: A flower with huge center garnet-colored stone is unsigned except for the "STERLING" mark. It measures 2" in diameter. $150.00 – 200.00.
Upper right: the golden topaz stone is a perfect complement to the gold washed STERLING setting. This brooch measures 3½" long. $75.00 – 125.00.
Lower middle: A massive brooch with purple stones. It measures a whopping 5½" tall and is not signed, and there is no sterling mark either. $150.00 – 200.00.

Beautiful birdcage brooch is suspended from a bow. The bird is mounted on a spring so that it moves with the wearer's movements. The brooch has delicate enameling with rhinestone accents and measures 3" tall x 2" at its widest. Signed "STARET" on a raised rectangle. $500.00 – 600.00.

This 2" tall circus bear was designed by Frank Gargano according to design patent number 147266 granted on August 12, 1947. Sapphire-colored and pavé-set crystal clear rhinestones embellish this beautiful pin. Faintly marked "STERLING." $125.00 – 175.00.

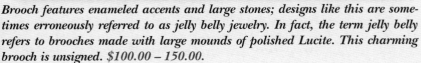

Brooch features enameled accents and large stones; designs like this are sometimes erroneously referred to as jelly belly jewelry. In fact, the term jelly belly refers to brooches made with large mounds of polished Lucite. This charming brooch is unsigned. $100.00 – 150.00.

Beautiful lyre with diamante trim measures 2½" tall x 2" at the widest. This piece is often referred to as Carnegie Hall jewelry in vintage advertisements, as the release of this line from Coro coincided with the release of the movie by the same name. It is signed "CoroCraft STERLING" with the Pegasus symbol on a raised rectangle, and matches patent no. 147183 issued to A. Katz on July 22, 1947. $250.00 – 300.00.

Rice-Weiner & Company designed this brooch named "Crystal Gazer." The brooch features gold-plated metal with enamel and Lucite which sold for $1.00 in 1940. Rice-Weiner held exclusive reproduction rights on designs inspired by the movie entitled **The Thief of Bagdad**. The brooch is signed "*THIEF OF BAGDAD KORDA©.*" The signature plate includes numbers 113 and 61 on the left and right of the signature, respectively. $175.00 – 225.00.

There were many designs in the line, including ornate brooches, bracelets, necklaces, rings, and earrings. In **American Costume Jewelry** by Carla Ginelli Brunialti and Roberto Brunialti, the authors note the line may have been designed by Louis C. Mark, who was the head designer for Rice-Weiner at the time.

This fabulous brooch features curled ribbons and dimensional flowers of gold vermeil over sterling. The Asian-inspired face appears to be carved out of a dark wood, but is actually plastic made to look like wood. It measures 2" long x 2¾" wide. This brooch matches patent #149497 issued May 4, 1948 and designed by Sylvia Hobé (See Figure 47). It is signed "Hobé 1/20 14K" over "STERLING" and "DESIGN PAT'D." $400.00 – 600.00.

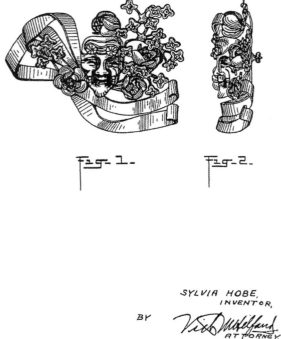

Figure 47: Patent for brooch pin or similar article granted to Sylvia Hobé on May 4, 1948.

Magnificent Eisenberg brooch, signed "EISENBERG ORIGINAL STERLING" with crystal color chatons, large and small. It measures 3½" x 3¼". $600.00 – 800.00.

Trifari fan brooch matches design patent 155199 (which is marked on the pin back). Graceful and flowing, the fan has a gentle curve to it; an exquisite piece. Signed "TRIFARI." $200.00 – 300.00.

Patriotic timepiece/brooch measures almost 4" long x 3" wide and has it all; eagle motif with watch — both popular in the early 1940s. Unsigned. $100.00 – 150.00.

Coro "Rock Fish" brooch features gold-plated sterling with enameled and rhinestone accents. It is marked "CoroCraft STERLING." The design is almost certainly the work of Gene Verri (Verrecchia) as he was the only designer for Coro from 1934 to 1946 and was still the head designer for the company when they closed their doors on December 27, 1979. The design has also been attributed to Adolph Katz (his name appeared on many design patents); however, Mr. Katz was an executive vice president of the Coro company and did not work in the design department per se.[18] This is a magnificent brooch but collectors should beware as fakes of this popular brooch abound. $400.00 – 600.00.

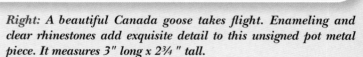

Right: A beautiful Canada goose takes flight. Enameling and clear rhinestones add exquisite detail to this unsigned pot metal piece. It measures 3" long x 2¾ " tall.

Lower left: Coro jelly belly is signed "Coro Craft" and "STERLING." It also features enameling and clear rhinestone accents, and matches patent number 137356 issued on February 22, 1944, to A. Katz (See Figure 48). $150.00 – 175.00 each.

Figure 48: Patent for brooch or similar article granted to A. Katz on February 22, 1944.

[18] See *Vintage Fashion & Costume Jewelry*, Vol. 19, No. 1, 2009.

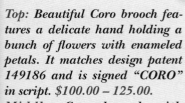

Top: Beautiful Coro brooch features a delicate hand holding a bunch of flowers with enameled petals. It matches design patent 149186 and is signed "CORO" in script. $100.00 – 125.00.

Middle: Coro brooch with intact hang tag reads "Styled to Beautify" and "Coro STERLING." It measures 4½" tall and is similar to design patent 132333 granted on May 5, 1942 (See Figure 49). $50.00 – 75.00.

Far right: Silver-tone brooch measures almost 5" tall and is stamped "STARET." $150.00 – 200.00.

Left: Rose and gold brooch is marked "VAN DELL 1/20th 12 KT GF." It measures 4" tall. $75.00 – 100.00.

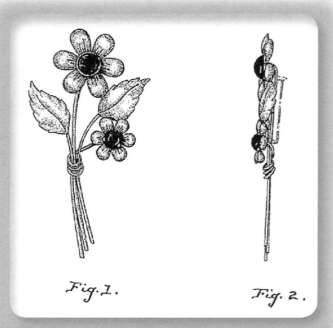

Figure 49: Patent granted to A. Katz on May 5, 1942.

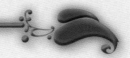

Fabulous floral brooch measures 5¼" long. Accents feature moonstones and clear rhinestones. It is unsigned. $100.00 – 150.00.

World War II-style brooch with flat pierced metal pin back with safety clasp. The brooch features gilt metal leaves and green glass beads and measures almost 5" in length. This is a Frank Hess design and as noted in the book **Miriam Haskell Jewelry** *by Cathy Gordon and Sheila Pamfiloff, Mr. Hess loved "dangles, beads hanging free form from a motif." Unsigned. $300.00 – 400.00.*

Trifari jelly belly brooch measures 2" wide x 2¼" high; it is marked "STERLING, TRIFARI" and "DES PAT NO 135188." $400.00 – 500.00.

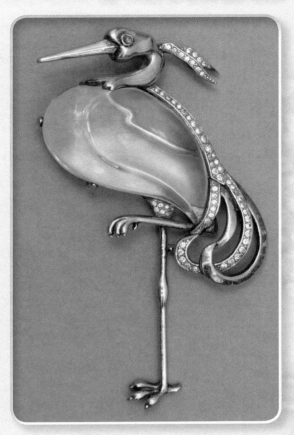

Magnificent heron jelly belly brooch measures 3¾" tall and matches design patent number 135175 granted on March 23, 1943 to A. Phillipe. $800.00 – 1,000.00.

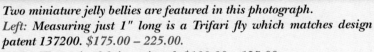

Two miniature jelly bellies are featured in this photograph.
Left: Measuring just 1" long is a Trifari fly which matches design patent 137200. $175.00 – 225.00.
Right: The petite fish is unsigned. $100.00 – 125.00.

"Freshie" jelly belly is a "college boy freshman" who was so named in a 1945 Women's Wear Daily advertisement. "His rakishly tilted cap and large bow tie make him a devil with the co-eds." This Elzac brooch sold for $4.50. Marked "STERLING." $300.00 – 400.00.

Magnificent enameled gazelle measures 3" at its widest and features clear rhinestone accents. It is marked "CoroCraft STERLING." $600.00 – 700.00.

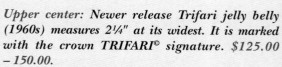

Upper center: Newer release Trifari jelly belly (1960s) measures 2¼" at its widest. It is marked with the crown TRIFARI© signature. $125.00 – 150.00.

Lower left: Famous Trifari rabbit jelly belly is marked "STERLING" and "TRIFARI" as well as "DES.PAT 135109." $300.00 – 400.00.

Right: A STERLING floral spray typical of the retro modern style. $100.00 – 125.00.

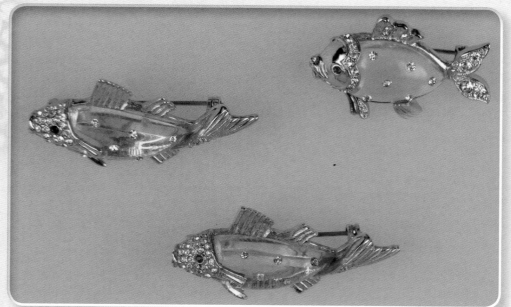

A school of Sea Imps by Coro. The ad reads "Coro's refreshing collection of fish pins. Lustrous Lucite setting studded with rhinestones — they'll be your accessory favorites for spring." (See Figure 50). Each is signed "Coro" on a raised rectangle. They match design patent 153696 granted on May 10, 1949. $150.00 – 200.00 each.

Figure 50: Coro Sea Imps advertisement features three styles of brooches; "Lustrous Lucite setting, studded with rhinestones..."

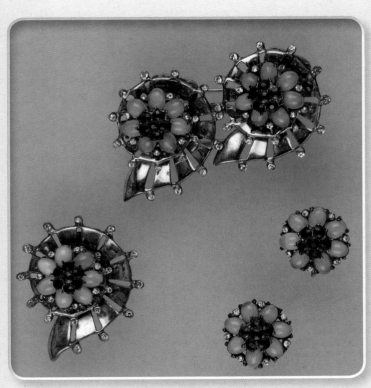

Fabulous Coro fur clip duette (also featured is an extra clip) and matching screw-back earrings match design patent 139102 which was granted to A. Katz on October 10, 1944. Each clip is marked "STERLING;" the duette mechanism is marked with the utility patent number 1798867 and "Coro Duette." Pale blue moonstones contrast beautifully with the ruby red rhinestones in a gold-plated setting. See Figure 51 for copy of the design patent. $300.00 – 400.00.

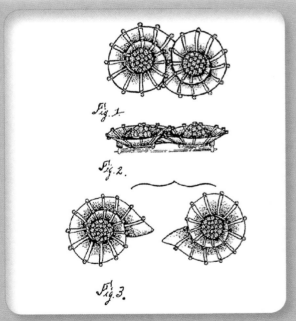

Fig.1.

Fig.2.

Fig.3.

Figure 51: Patent for separable brooch granted to A. Katz on October 10, 1944.

Coro Sterling duette features matching earrings. Each clip is marked "STERLING" and one owl is marked "STERLING CoroCraft." This set, named "Hoots," matches design patent 138960, which was granted on October 3, 1944 to A. Katz. Two additional utility patent numbers can be found on the duette and earrings, including 1798867 (duette) and 1967965 (earrings). See Figure 52 for copy of design patent. $300.00 – 400.00.

Figure 52: Copy of design patent 138960.

Penguins were a popular motif and were marketed by several companies. This is a pair of fur clips, perhaps "Mr. and Mrs." They measure just 1½" high, slightly larger for Mr. Penguin. The plastic pearl bodies and enameled accents are in excellent condition, given the age of this whimsical pair. $200.00 – 300.00.

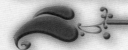

Left: A demure wishbone with rose matches design patent 149359. It is signed "Coro." $35.00 – 50.00. Right: Lucky wishbone brooch features delicate cabochons, pearls, and rhinestones. The dangling heart is marked "Coro STERLING" and the pin is marked on an oval cartouche "STERLING by Coro." It matches design patent 141117 granted on May 8, 1945 to A. Katz. See Figure 53 for copy of design patent. $50.00 – 75.00.

Figure 53: Patent for brooch pin granted to A. Katz on May 8, 1945.

Figure 54: Patent for brooch or similar article granted to A. Katz on September 8, 1942.

Imposing brooch from Coro measures almost 3" x 4" tall. Clear rhinestone and enameled accents are featured; this matches design patent 133730 issued September 8, 1942 (see Figure 54). It is signed "Coro Craft STERLING." $400.00 – 500.00.

Although this large brooch is unsigned, it matches design patent 128822 issued on August 12, 1941 to A. Katz (see Figure 55). It is a gold-plated metal fur clip, measures 5" tall, and is beautifully accented with clear and colored rhinestones as well as enameling. $300.00 – 400.00.

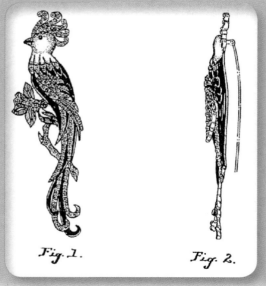

Figure 55: Patent for pin clip granted to A. Katz on August 12, 1941.

The design of this pot metal brooch is based on the drawings of Berta Hummel. Several versions of this pin exist, some without enamel accents, others with more color variations. The brooch measures almost 3" tall. Unsigned. $125.00 – 175.00.

The "Hummelchen" (little Bumblebee) was Berta's nickname. She was born on May 21, 1909, at Massing am Rott in Bavaria. She became a nun at age 25 and lived at the Franciscan Abbey of Siessen in Germany until her premature death in 1946. Her artistic ability was already well recognized by the time she entered the Abbey. Today, Hummel figurines remain some of the most popular collectibles ever made.

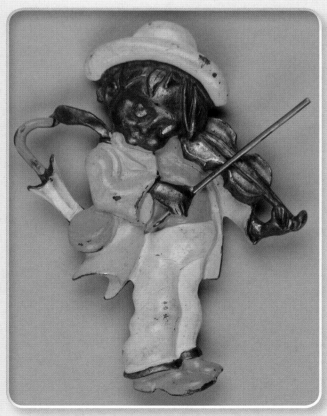

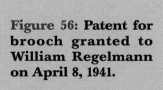

Figure 56: Patent for brooch granted to William Regelmann on April 8, 1941.

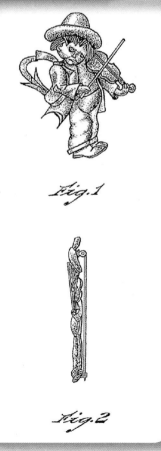

The design of this pot metal brooch is based on the drawings of Berta Hummel and several versions of this pin also exist. The design patent for this brooch is number 126405 issued to William Regelmann on April 8, 1941 (see Figure 56). Unsigned. $125.00 – 175.00.

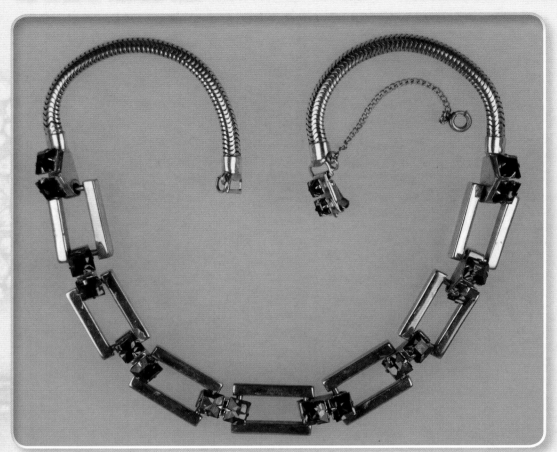

Classic example of retro modern design features snake chain and rhinestone detail on the clasp. Unsigned. $75.00 – 100.00.

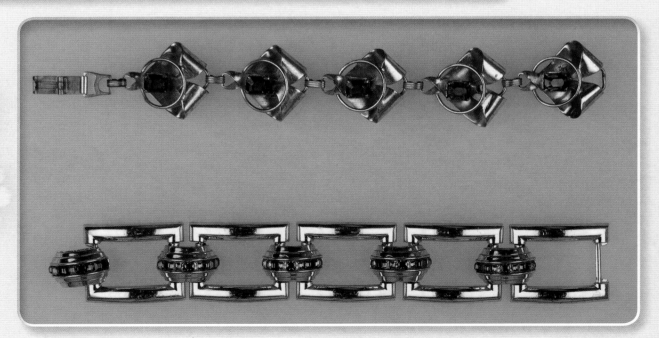

Top: Bracelet was manufactured by Rice-Weiner for McClelland Barclay. It is signed "Barclay" and "STERLING." $200.00 – 300.00.

Bottom: Bracelet is signed "Coro" in script and features channel set blue stones in a lovely retro design. When the clasp is closed, you cannot tell where it is as the design is continuous. $75.00 – 100.00.

Elzac brooches were made of heavily carved wood and ceramic and embellished with almost every imaginable material.[19] The company flourished even with the labor shortages and material problems associated with the war.

In fact, they were having trouble keeping up with the demand for their products. When they could not count on subcontractors to provide parts or sub-assemblies, the company established a complete manufacturing plant which occupied four floors and the basements of two adjoining buildings. Clay mixing machines and electric and gas kilns were located in the basements; on the next floors, row after row of employees hand embellished and painted the novelty figures, flowers, and ceramic jewelry items.

The company employed a novel, direct-from-the-factory-to-retailer system that had showrooms located strategically in the Midwest, South, Great Lakes, and New York regions, as well as Los Angeles. According to company records, Elzac Novelty Jewelry was sold in Cuba, Hawaii, and Central and South America as well as the continental United States. Many Elzac designs were patented to protect them from competitors. Today these provide an important and historic record for collectors. Some designs that were not patented were captured in Elliot Handler's sketches and provide a unique glimpse into the designs of Elzac.

Many of the company's records, legal agreements, pho-

Everyone has heard of Barbie® dolls. Since her debut at the New York City American Toy Fair in 1959, Barbie has become a toy icon. Creators Ruth and Elliot Handler modeled Barbie after a German design and co-founded Mattel with their former employee, Harold Mattson, to produce the doll. Before Barbie, the Handlers were part of the company named Elzac of Hollywood. In its heyday, the multi-million dollar Elzac business employed over 400 people. That number included more than a dozen ceramic sculptors and nearly as many wood carvers. Partner Zemby wanted to step up the business so he brought in additional partners in mid-1942. Handler was getting restless and wanted to expand into other product lines, including toys. The partners resisted Handler's ideas so he asked to be bought out of the company. By October of 1944 he was. History reveals that the Handlers' success story continued. Today, every three seconds, someone, somewhere buys a Barbie doll!

tographs, and design sketches were donated by the Handlers to the Schlesinger Library at Radcliffe Institute, Harvard University, before Mrs. Handler's death in 2002. The documents and sketches provide a wonderful view into the workings of the company, the employees, and the artistic renderings of a gifted artist, Elliot Handler.

Figure 57: Elzac factory workers are making brooches from wood. Courtesy of the Handlers and the Schlesinger Library at Radcliffe Institute, Harvard University.

Figure 58: Elzac factory workers are shown adding detail to refine wooden brooches. Courtesy of the Handlers and the Schlesinger Library at Radcliffe Institute, Harvard University.

[19] Note: Elzac brooches made from wood are included in the section on wooden jewelry.

Figure 59: Women working in the Elzac factory are adding trim to the ceramic brooches. Courtesy of the Handlers and the Schlesinger Library at Radcliffe Institute, Harvard University.

Figure 60: Women working in the Elzac factory are adding trim to ceramic brooches. Courtesy of the Handlers and the Schlesinger Library at Radcliffe Institute, Harvard University.

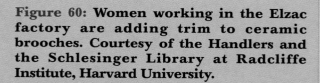

Figure 61: Elzac factory worker is shown putting trays in the kiln to fire ceramic brooches. Courtesy of the Handlers and the Schlesinger Library at Radcliffe Institute, Harvard University.

Ceramic Eskimo twins feature one with open eyes, the other with eyes shut. The twins are mounted on a wood backing for added support. Fur trim, unsigned. $150.00 – 200.00.

Pompadoured pottery belle has hat and trimmings of red cellophane. This lovely lady was featured in a Lit Brothers advertisement (see Figure 62) and sold for $1.69 plus tax. Price now, $125.00 – 175.00.

$1.69

Plus Federal Tax

New Ceramic Heads

Wear this pompadoured pottery belle for newness! She's wearing a hat and trimmings of red cellophane. Just one of many pins at this price!

Other Pins, $1.69 to $49.95

Figure 62: Lit Brothers store ad for Elzac pompadoured pottery belle.

195

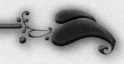

Unusual Elzac brooch features a large metal headdress. It measures 2½" wide x 4" long. $125.00 – 175.00.

Figure 63: Elliot Handler sketches showing designs for Elzac brooches. Courtesy of the Schlesinger Library, Radcliffe Institute, Harvard University.

Straight from Elliot Handler's drawing board (See Figure 63), This "Bunnykins" brooch features colored Lucite accents. $125.00 – 175.00.

A dramatic sweep of Lucite and jeweled hat dress up this lovely Elzac brooch which measures almost 5" long. $150.00 – 200.00.

Elzac brooch features braided cord trim and fancy Lucite headdress. $150.00 – 200.00.

Upper left and upper right: recognizable Elzac Bonnet Head brooches. $125.00 – 175.00 each. Bottom: blue and yellow make a striking color combination in this Elzac piece with earrings. $125.00 – 175.00.

An unlikely duo features an innocent looking "Daisy" on the left with pigtails and ribbons; on the right, "Madame X" – a mysterious lady with yellow braid and pom pom hat. Note the red Lucite bow tied under her chin. The design for Daisy was patented (see Figure 64 while Madame X was featured in a Sears ad (see Figure 65). Daisy, $150.00 – 200.00; Madame X, $125.00 – 175.00.

Sears ad reprinted with permission from "Everyday Fashions of the Forties As Pictured in Sears Catalogs," Dover Publications, Inc., 31 East Second Street, Mineola, NY, 11501.

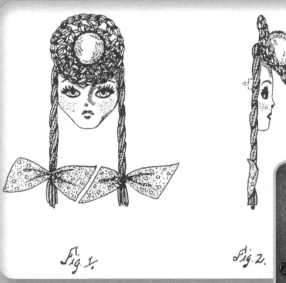

Figure 64: Patent for ceramic brooch pin granted to Elliot Handler on August 24, 1943.

Lapel "Pin-ups" in gay hand-painted ceramics

12 styles **85c** Each

For your lapel . . . whimsical animals, shy fawns, impish monkeys and many other pets in fun-provoking poses. Bizarre masks, too! They're conversation makers wherever worn, and so low priced you'll want several. Made of ceramic with hand painted colors: luscious reds, vivid greens, soft blues, yellow and white. Trimmed with bits of leather, plastic Lucite, yarn and beads. Make grand gifts. Clever pin-ups for bedroom or kitchen curtains too. Individually gift boxed. Shpg. wt., each, 4 oz.

[A] 4 K 3777E—HOBBY. Prancing thoroughbred with flying green mane and tail. Brown body. 3 inches high 85c
[B] 4 K 3774E—BAMBI. Dear little fawn with soft-blue body and white spots. Pink Lucite ears. 2¼ in. high 85c
[C] 4 K 3773E—ELIZA. A belle with clear Lucite hat tilted over her eye. Orange color flower trim. 3½ in. high . 85c
[D] 4 K 3764E—BUNKY. Mischievous little white monkey with tiny button cap. Purple Lucite tail. 2¾ in. high . 85c
[E] 4 K 3772E—WUMPIE. Whimsical giraffe with nodding head. Red Lucite spring neck. Yellow body with green spots. 3½ inches high. Smart on sweaters 85c
[F] 4 K 3763E—SHEIK. Arabian chieftain. Head swathed in yarn turban (variegated colors). 3¼ inches high 85c
[G] 4 K 3779E—MADAME X. Mysterious lady with yellow braid and red yarn pompon hat. Red Lucite bow tied under her chin. 3¼ inches high 85c
[H] 4 K 3775E—MARY'S LAMB wears pink bonnet tied under her chin, carries purple leather purse. 4 in. high 85c
[J] 4 K 3770E—PEGASUS. Mythical flying horse with wings of clear Lucite. Green body. 3½ inches high 85c
[K] 4 K 3778E—CAROL ANN. Shy little miss with red felt hat, green dress, yellow pigtails. 2½ in. high 85c
[L] 4 K 3769E—TEXAS STEER. Outthrust green Lucite horns. Brown leather ears. Brown wood face. 3 in. high . . . 85c
[M] 4 K 3768E—BONNIE. Demure little lamb wears orange pompon bonnet with blue bead trim. 2¾ inches high . 85c

Figure 65: Advertisement from Sears catalog (1944 – 1945) showing a variety of Elzac brooches called "lapel 'pin-ups' in gay hand painted ceramics." Reprinted with permission of Dover Publications, Inc.

Left: Highly embellished "black face" brooch is finished with felt turban. $150.00 – 200.00.
Right: Native princess pin features felt turban held together with a colored toothpick; note the bold earrings and curly hair. $150.00 – 200.00.

Top: Pegasus, mythical flying horse with wings of clear Lucite. Measuring 3¼" high, this brooch originally sold for 85¢. Price today, $125.00 – 175.00.
Bottom: Bunky the mischievous little monkey pin; in the Sears ad, Bunky was white with a purple Lucite tail. $125.00 – 175.00.

Demure "Bonnie" brooch wears a pom pom bonnet with bead trim. $125.00 – 175.00.

Rhinestones

Lovely brooch features large green cabochons and aurora borealis rhinestone accents in a heavy gold-tone setting. It measures 2" wide x 1½" from top to bottom. Signed "SPINX," it also has a design number. $50.00 – 75.00.

Beautiful and lightweight brooch features a variety of molded stones which are glued in; all other stones are prong set. The brooch is large and measures 3" wide x 1½" from top to bottom. Unsigned. $75.00 – 125.00.

Juliana brooch features characteristic open back stones; all are prong set. Juliana jewelry was marked with paper hang tags which were removed before wearing. Today, Juliana jewelry is identified by characteristic construction elements (see Buyer's Table in the back of the book). Unsigned. $75.00 – 125.00.

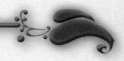

This Regency brooch is massive and measures 4½" long. It features a variety of beautiful green and aurora borealis rhinestones in an antiqued gold-tone setting, as well as a beautiful art stone nestled in the center. Signed "REGENCY" on an oval cartouche. $100.00 – 150.00.

Top: This brooch features Venetian inspired stones with copper accents. It measures almost 2" x 2". Unsigned. $50.00 – 75.00.
Bottom: Lightweight brooch featuring large red and root beer colored rhinestones with aurora borealis accents. Unsigned but featuring the lightweight construction characteristic of Beau Jewels. $75.00 – 100.00.

Lightweight construction is again featured in this lovely brooch featuring golden and smoky topaz colored rhinestones, all prong set. It measures 2¼" across x 1¾" high. Unsigned but featuring the lightweight construction characteristic of Beau Jewels. $75.00 – 100.00.

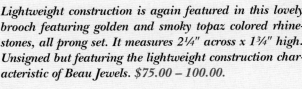

Wear this as a pin or pendant, take your pick. This lovely domed brooch features golden topaz and citrine colored stones in a gold-tone setting. A very dimensional piece, it is signed "Capri©" on a raised rectangle. $75.00 – 125.00.

A modified Maltese cross design, this brooch measures 2¼" x 2¼". It features large smoked topaz colored stones with citrine stones as accents. All are prong set in this lovely unsigned piece. $75.00 – 100.00.

Weiss brooch still has its original price tag; would you believe this stunning brooch featuring smoked topaz baguettes accented by dozens of prong-set clear stones originally cost $2.00? It is not signed, but stamped with the crown symbol which is also featured on the price tag. It measures almost 4" in length. $100.00 – 125.00.

Classic Juliana styling by DeLizza & Elster is revealed in this wonderful brooch with slim, open backed olivine navettes. Measuring almost 3" in diameter, it is unsigned. $125.00 – 150.00.

Long and slender describes these two lovely brooches.
Left: Classic Trifari scepter with large pear shaped clear stone is from the 1953 Coronation Gems series which coincided with the coronation of Queen Elizabeth II. The brooch measures 4¼" tall and is stamped "TRIFARI" with crown symbol. $125.00 – 150.00.
Right: A favorite Sarah Coventry brooch measuring 5" in length. The large prong-set, smoked topaz marquis at the top measures 1" long. Signed "©SARAHCOV." $75.00 – 100.00.

Top: DeLizza & Elster artistry is once again on display in this lovely blue and green brooch at the top. The brooch features open backed stones in a shiny rhodium setting accented by a huge rose cut chaton. Overall the brooch measures 2" wide x 1¾" high. Unsigned. $75.00 – 100.00.
Bottom: A magnificent layered brooch features dozens of clear and aurora borealis stones, all prong set. Six flowers sit on top of the base for a dimensional effect in this Juliana brooch by DeLizza & Elster. A very heavy brooch, it is unsigned and measures 3" at its widest points. $100.00 – 125.00.

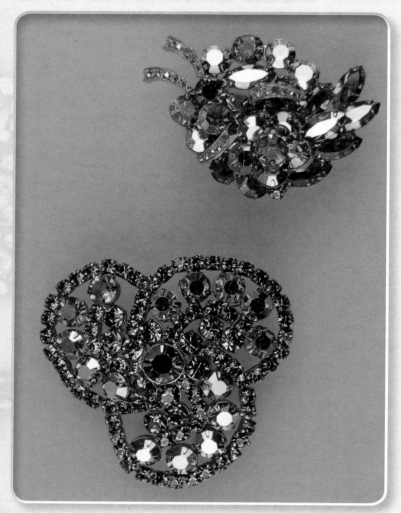

Top: Icy pink aurora borealis chatons and navettes create a dazzling effect in this brooch. It features ribbons of rhinestones, also known as icing, often seen in Eisenberg designs. However, this brooch is unsigned. $75.00 – 100.00.
Bottom: Brooch, shimmering champagne color is accented with aurora borealis chatons. It measures 3" at its widest. Unsigned, Juliana. $75.00 – 125.00.

Classic ART brooch measures 2" in diameter and features a variety of beautifully colored stones glued into the antiqued gold-tone setting. Signed "ART©" on a raised rectangle. $100.00 – 125.00.

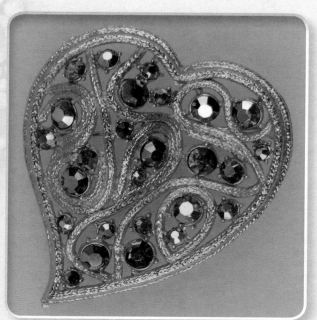

This heart pin has a wavy surface and features sparkling aurora borealis stones; at its widest point it measures 3". Unsigned. $50.00 – 75.00.

Classic Juliana brooch by DeLizza & Elster features a massive rose cut tourmaline watermelon chaton as the focal point of this layered brooch. The navettes encircling the center stone measure a full 1" long. The center chaton is also an inch in diameter. Massive, 3" in diameter. $250.00 – 300.00.

Juliana brooch measures almost 3" in diameter and features a lovely blue/green color combination. All stones are prong set except the small emerald chatons. $175.00 – 225.00.

This massive and heavy Maltese cross can be worn as a pendant or pin. It measures almost 4" at its widest and features massive aurora borealis chatons and oval stones as the focal point. A spectacular brooch, unsigned. $150.00 – 200.00.

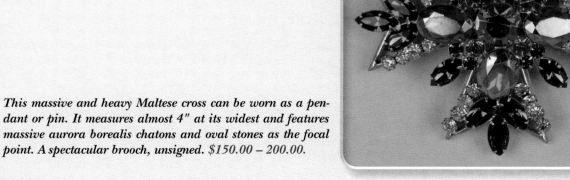

Giant clear rhinestones make up this heart brooch which is set in shiny rhodium. It measures 2" x 2" at its widest. Unsigned. $50.00 – 75.00.

I love white jewelry and this pin is no exception. Signed "WEISS" on an oval cartouche, this lovely piece features opaque white stones in various shapes as well as fancy nugget topped stones. Aurora borealis chatons provide the finishing touch. Weiss jewelry has been reproduced and the fakes are readily available in the collectibles market. The copies cannot compare to the real thing but collectors should be aware that poor quality fakes are plentiful. $50.00 – 75.00.

Magnificent brooch features a variety of crystal clear stones throughout. It is signed "KRAMER of NEW YORK" on an oval cartouche and measures 3½" at its widest x 2½" from top to bottom. The shiny rhodium setting looks like it was made yesterday. $100.00 – 125.00.

This brooch measures 3" in diameter and features a number of differently shaped crystal clear stones, including the small pear shaped stones that encircle the brooch. Five layers deep, this brooch measures over 1" in depth. Every single stone in this stunning piece is prong set. Signed "WEISS." $200.00 – 300.00.

Massive is the only way to describe this dimensional brooch set in shiny rhodium. It can barely fit in the palm of my hand and measures 4" in diameter! Unsigned. $200.00 – 300.00.

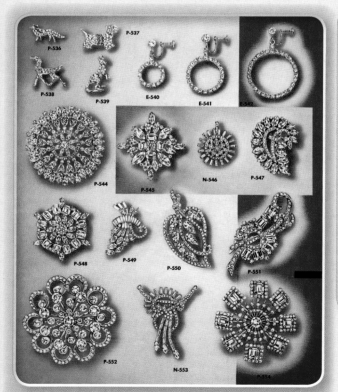

Figure 66: Page 3 from Jewel Creations company catalog showing the variety of brooches and earrings that could be made at home.

The Jewel Creations Company from Newark, New Jersey, sold jewelry kits and accessories. The advertising was geared toward women who could create and sell custom made jewelry from home. I believe both of these brooches are kit jewelry; the one on the right is featured in an undated Jewel Creations catalog (see Figure 66). As you can see, the jewelry is beautiful.
Left: The aurora borealis stones are set in shiny gold tone and the pin measures 2½" in diameter. $50.00 – 75.00.
Right: Clear stones are set in a shiny silver-tone setting; this pin also measures 2½" in diameter. Unsigned. $50.00 – 75.00.

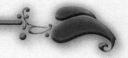

Dozens of aurora borealis chatons are prong set in this shiny gold-tone setting which measures 3" x 3½" wide. Unsigned. $100.00 – 125.00.

Beautiful Miriam Haskell brooch features rows of Niki seed pearls on gold-plated filigree back and is very likely the work of designer Robert Clark. It is often difficult to date Haskell jewelry because the various owners of the company worked to perpetuate the original forms of the jewelry and "no successful design or construction device was ever abandoned."[20] Signed "MIRIAM HASKELL" on an oval cartouche. $300.00 – 400.00.

Magnificent layered brooch is also characteristic of the Robert Clark era. Large center baroque pearl is surrounded by rows of pearls and golden leaves set onto a filigree background. Measuring 2½" in diameter, this is signed "MIRIAM HASKELL" on an oval cartouche. $300.00 – 400.00.

[20] See page 194 in *Miriam Haskell Jewelry* by Cathy Gordon and Sheila Pamfiloff, Schiffer Publishing, 2004.

Large baroque pearl is nestled among golden leaves trimmed with Niki pearls in this brooch which also features clear prong-set rhinestones encircling the four smaller pearls. Layered and dimensional, it measures 3½" at widest diameter. Featuring Robert Clark design characteristics, this brooch is signed *"MIRIAM HASKELL"* on an oval cartouche. $300.00 – 400.00.

Massive floral piece features a baroque pearl encircled with clear, prong-set rhinestones in the flower and pearlized leaves on the flower stem. This brooch measures almost 4" long; you can see the gold filigree setting in the flower. Signed *"MIRIAM HASKELL"* on an oval cartouche. $200.00 – 300.00.

Lustrous faux pearls hang from the extended branches of this gold-plated dimensional brooch which measures 2½" tall. A classic Hobé design, it is signed accordingly on an oval cartouche. $100.00 – 150.00.

Miriam Haskell brooch features faux lapis and amethyst colored stones in a filigree setting. It measures 2¾" at its widest and is signed "MIRIAM HASKELL" on an oval cartouche. $200.00 – 300.00.

Maltese cross design is featured in this gold-tone brooch with cord trim. It measures 2¾" at its widest and is unsigned. $35.00 – 50.00.

Enameled accents and center cabochon decorate this petite brooch which measures just shy of 2" wide. Signed "ART©." $35.00 – 50.00.

Faux emeralds and rubies are accented with pearls in
this Renaissance Revival-style brooch signed "Capri©."
It measures 2" in diameter. $35.00 – 50.00.

Maltese cross design features tiny turquoise cabochons
and a large center pearl. This lovely brooch measures
2½" at its widest and is unsigned. $35.00 – 50.00.

Turquoise cabochons are accented with sapphires
in this swirled design. It measures 1¾" in diameter and is signed "KRAMER©." $50.00 – 75.00.

Upper middle: Brooch features a gold-tone setting and cabochon center. Signed "DeNicola©." $50.00 – 75.00.

Lower left: Faux turquoise, lapis, and white cabochons are featured in this domed brooch. It is signed "JOMAZ©." $50.00 – 75.00.

Lower right: Hand-wrapped flower features faux turquoise cabochons. This brooch is signed "DeNicola" without the copyright symbol. $100.00 – 150.00.

Left: Mimi di Niscemi gold-tone brooch is signed "Mimi d N" and is dated 1985; her well-made jewelry is somewhat rare in the collectibles market, but fortunately for collectors it is easy to identify and date. $50.00 – 75.00.

Right: Fun brooch is classic Goldette with intricate designs featuring small stones (faux turquoise, ruby, and pearl in this case). Note the coiled snake on one post and the fly on another. Signed "Goldette©." $50.00 – 75.00.

In her delightful book entitled **Read My Pins,** *Madeleine Albright, who served as both U. S. Ambassador to the United Nations and Secretary of State during the Clinton administration, describes occasions when diplomatic negotiations proceeded more slowly than she hoped. She stocked up on turtles to signify her impatience. Mrs. Albright says that jewelry became an important part of her personal diplomatic arsenal. She noted that former President George H. Bush had been known for saying "Read my lips," and during her diplomatic tenure, she began urging colleagues and reporters to "Read my pins." I love the idea of nonverbal communication via jewelry. I've stocked up on turtles to signify my impatience at the pace at which my children pick up their rooms and do their homework. But I digress…*

Left: Beautiful turtle brooch by Adele Simpson. Ms. Simpson was a fashion designer who also sold boutique-quality costume jewelry to complement her clothing line. Signed "Adele Simpson" on a raised rectangle, this brooch measures 2¼" in length. $100.00 – 150.00.

Right: Ruby red and pink stones complement the center art stone in this unsigned brooch. $100.00 – 125.00.

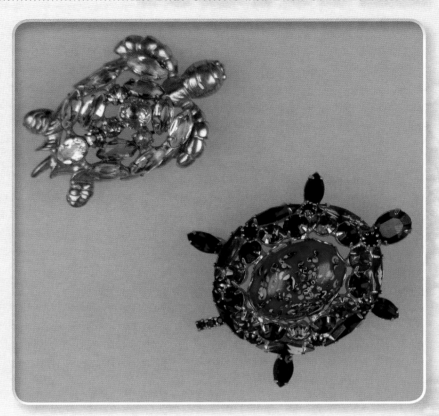

Left: Magnificent rose cut oval center stone dominates this petite pin; pale lavender stones encircle the body for a dazzling yet subtle effect. Unsigned, measuring just almost 2" long. $100.00 – 125.00.

Right: Brown enameling complements the center faux jade shell of this pretty gold-tone turtle brooch from Ciner. Signed "CINER." $250.00 – 300.00.

Light: This fancy turtle, signed "ART©," has lots of pretty details including enameled and rhinestone studded flowers. It measures 2" long. $75.00 – 100.00. Right: Faux turquoise oval cabochon is encircled with pretty purple navettes and chatons for maximum impact in this colorful, unsigned brooch. $100.00 – 125.00.

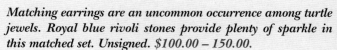

Matching earrings are an uncommon occurrence among turtle jewels. Royal blue rivoli stones provide plenty of sparkle in this matched set. Unsigned. $100.00 – 150.00.

Mrs. Albright's collection of turtle brooches includes these two massive fellows. Each measures a whopping 3" wide x 4" long and is trimmed with crystal clear stones. Unsigned. $100.00 – 125.00.

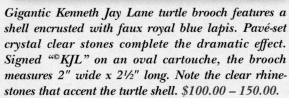

Gigantic Kenneth Jay Lane turtle brooch features a shell encrusted with faux royal blue lapis. Pavé-set crystal clear stones complete the dramatic effect. Signed "©KJL" on an oval cartouche, the brooch measures 2" wide x 2½" long. Note the clear rhinestones that accent the turtle shell. $100.00 – 150.00.

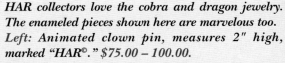

HAR collectors love the cobra and dragon jewelry. The enameled pieces shown here are marvelous too.
Left: Animated clown pin, measures 2" high, marked "HAR©." $75.00 – 100.00.
Right: A happy hobo brooch looking for a handout, measures 2" high, marked "HAR©." $75.00 – 100.00.

The colorful chubby clown on this pin is holding a bouquet of rhinestone encrusted flowers with pearl centers. A very dimensional piece, he measures 3" tall. Signed "JOMAZ©," this type of figural jewelry is very popular with collectors. $200.00 – 250.00.

A popular design by Kenneth Jay Lane features enameled body decorated with clear rhinestones. Faux pearl face adds a delightful touch to this clown who is perched perilously on a pearl, measures 2¾" tall, and is signed "KJL©." $150.00 – 200.00.

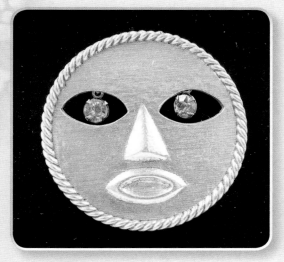

Popular Pauline Rader brooch features dangling crystal clear chatons for the eyes. It measures 1¾" in diamteter and is signed on an oval cartouche. $50.00 – 75.00.

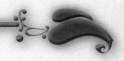

Left: Asian-inspired figural brooch with detailed turban, faux jade cabochons, and clear stones. The face is plastic. Signed "Nettie Rosenstein" on an elongated oval cartouche, this type of figural jewelry is rare and very collectible. The pin measures 1¾" tall. $200.00 – 250.00.
Right: Beautifully enameled brooch by ART measures 2¼" tall. Signed "ART©." $75.00 – 100.00.

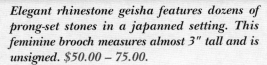

Elegant rhinestone geisha features dozens of prong-set stones in a japanned setting. This feminine brooch measures almost 3" tall and is unsigned. $50.00 – 75.00.

King and queen brooch pair features prong-set marquis and square-cut Siam rhinestones with iridescent cabochon faces. The King holds a scepter with heart shaped stone; the queen has moveable earrings. All stones except for the facial cabochons are prong set. King measures 2½" tall; the queen is slightly shorter at 2" tall. The pair is unsigned. $150.00 – 200.00.

Left: A large bird brooch with enameled head and turquoise cabochons set in gold stone. This magnificent brooch measures 3½" tall and is signed "©BOUCHER" with the design number. $400.00 – 500.00.
Right: 1960s Boucher phoenix bird is decorated with light sapphire and chrysoprase cabochon stones with Siam and clear rhinestones. This is a massive brooch measuring 4¼" x 3¼". Signed "©BOUCHER" with the design number. $700.00 – 800.00.

Almost identical settings are featured in these contemporary bird brooches. The right brooch's bright enameling and clear stones in the tail turn a bold design into downright showy. Both are unsigned and measure a whopping 5" tall. $50.00 – 75.00 each.

A sweeping tail lends grace to this elegant peacock pin which measures 4" long. The abundance of clear rhinestones and colorful cabochons lend additional beauty to this signed piece. However, I cannot make out the signature. $75.00 – 100.00.

Ruby red stones are pavé set on the body of this otherwise enameled peacock. This newer piece measures 2½" in diameter and is unsigned. $35.00 – 50.00.

Left: I love the pearls that adorn this peacock. Combined with the sapphire colored stones, the effect is very dramatic. Measures about 1½" wide x 2½" long. Unsigned. $35.00 – 50.00.

Right: The colorful tail on this pin is achieved through enameled accents and clear rhinestones. Measures about 1½" wide x 2½" long. Unsigned. $35.00 – 60.00.

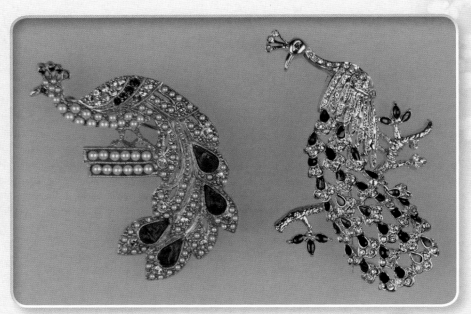

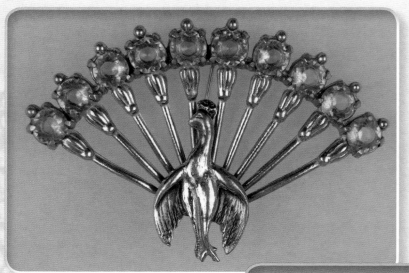

Pot metal peacock from the 1930s features a single row of blue stones with a touch of blue enameling. It measures 3¼" at widest x 2¼" tall. Unsigned. $100.00 – 125.00.

Above left: Pretty enameling and clear stones highlight the details in this pair of parrots. Sapphire chatons are used for the eyes and pick up the blue color on the birds' wings. Signed "LR" in script. The mark is for Lady Remington, first known as ACT II jewelry. The name was changed to Lady Remington when the company was acquired by Victor Kiam in 1986. The company is now known as Lia Sophia Jewelry and is a direct sales organization. Lia and Sophia are the granddaughters of Kiam; his son Tory is the president. $50.00 – 75.00.
Above right: A dimensional bird features pretty enameling and clear rhinestone accents. The depth of the bird is almost 1", achieved with two pieces that are riveted together. It is signed "©D'Orlan." $50.00 – 75.00.

This feathery friend has enameled detailing and measures 3" tall. Similar brooches are often signed "Hattie Carnegie," although this one is unsigned. $50.00 – 75.00.

*Left: This playful tiger pin is signed "POLCINI©"
and measures 2" wide. $50.00 – 75.00.*
*Right: This lion brooch who is winking at the
observer is signed "©BOUCHER" with no inven-
tory number. $50.00 – 75.00.*

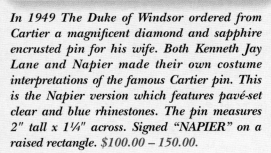

*In 1949 The Duke of Windsor ordered from
Cartier a magnificent diamond and sapphire
encrusted pin for his wife. Both Kenneth Jay
Lane and Napier made their own costume
interpretations of the famous Cartier pin. This
is the Napier version which features pavé-set
clear and blue rhinestones. The pin measures
2" tall x 1¼" across. Signed "NAPIER" on a
raised rectangle. $100.00 – 150.00.*

**Chinese lion brooch features antiqued gold-tone setting
with pavé rhinestones, ruby red cabochon eyes, and
enameled trim. This brooch measures 3" tall and is
attributed to Kenneth Jay Lane. $300.00 – 400.00.**

Nylon adorns this fish which also features an emerald cabochon for the eye and enameled details including those fabulous pink lips. Signed "Hattie Carnegie" on an oval cartouche, the brooch measures 3½" wide x 2" high. $200.00 – 300.00.

Details on this domed, gold-tone fish include pavé-set clear stones and a Siam colored cabochon for the eye. This unsigned piece measures 2¾" wide x 2" high. $35.00 – 60.00.

Gold filigree setting with colorful stones make this fish a wonderful catch. It can be worn as a pendant or brooch and is signed "MADE IN GERMANY WEST" on a cartouche. $50.00 – 75.00.

Unsigned pot metal lobster brooch features gigantic stones that comprise the body of this collectible crustacean. Measuring 3½" x 2½", the gold-plated metal brooch also features red enameled detail and rhinestones. The claws on this version are fixed. Unsigned. $200.00 – 300.00.

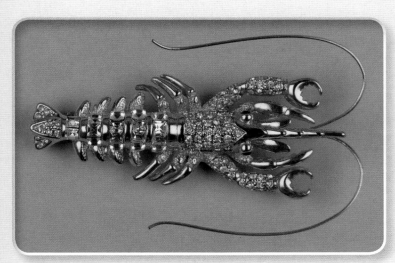

This beautiful lobster brooch in gold tone is lavishly decorated with clear stones, both pavé and channel set. Emerald green cabochons for the eyes add a touch of color. Unsigned. $50.00 – 75.00.

Coral colored enameling contrasts beautifully with the turquoise and pearl accents on this Trifari seahorse pin which measures 3" tall. It is signed with the "Crown Trifari©" signature on a raised rectangle. $300.00 – 400.00.

From the 1980s comes this articulated lizard brooch with two pin mechanisms. Measuring a full 5" long, these were often worn on the shoulder or back. Unsigned. $75.00 – 125.00.

Pretty pavé-set rhinestones belie the danger that lies within the toothy jaws of this alligator. With open mouth this critter is 1" deep and almost 3" long. Unsigned. $50.00 – 75.00.

Ann Pitman's books[21] always include funny anecdotes about her own jewelry. She has a similar snake brooch and says she wears it everywhere, except to church. Measuring a full 5½" long, this serpent has dozens of prong-set stones. I looked everywhere for a Butler and Wilson signature, but this is unsigned. $100.00 – 150.00.

[21] Pitman, Ann. *Inside the Jewelry Box: A Collector's Guide to Costume Jewelry.* Collector Books, Paducah, KY, 2004.

I looked all over this dragon brooch for a Butler and Wilson signature also; it is definitely their design. Metallic enamel accents and pavé-set rhinestones decorate this enormous 1980s – 1990s brooch that measures 5½" long with a depth of 1½". This one should be worn on a jacket or coat to support its weight. Unsigned. $150.00 – 200.00.

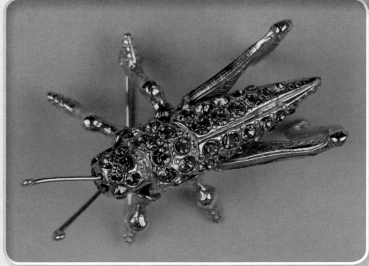

Talk about dimensional, this grasshopper brooch, signed "MADE IN MEXICO," features glued-in golden topaz rhinestones in a shiny setting. The depth of this is almost 2" x 2½" long. It's surprisingly lightweight so it can be worn on a dress or jacket. $35.00 – 50.00.

Frog brooches always remind me of my son, who collected as many live frogs as he could get his hands on when he was a little boy. I often found their petrified remains in his bedroom. This colorful enameled fellow is trimmed with clear rhinestones and holds a smoked topaz cabochon in his webbed hands. He measures 2" x 2" and is signed "ART©." $50.00 – 75.00.
Always check the condition of the enamel on pieces like these as it can be susceptible to cracking.

Signed *"JEANNE©,"* this prancing mule pin with faux turquoise pendant and clear rhinestone trim measures 2" x 2". $50.00 – 75.00.

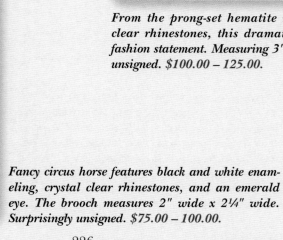

From the prong-set hematite navettes to the dozens of clear rhinestones, this dramatic horse brooch makes a fashion statement. Measuring 3" x 4", this massive piece is unsigned. $100.00 – 125.00.

Fancy circus horse features black and white enameling, crystal clear rhinestones, and an emerald eye. The brooch measures 2" wide x 2¼" wide. Surprisingly unsigned. $75.00 – 100.00.

Understated beauty is how I would describe this gold-tone horse brooch. Signed "NAPIER" without a © mark, it measures 2" x 2". $50.00 – 75.00.

Scarecrow signed "JEANNE©" features a large, misshapen pearl for its face. It measures 2¾" tall. $100.00 – 150.00.

Shiny gold-plated scarecrow marked "JBK" (for Camrose & Kross) measures 2½" tall clear rhinestones and colorful cabochon accents. $75.00 – 125.00.

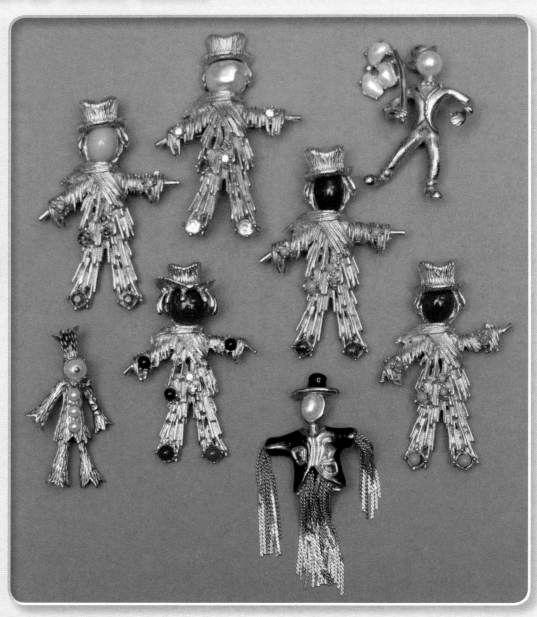

Collection of scarecrow brooches.

From upper left to right: Faux turquoise cabochon face and scarf adorn this unsigned piece which measures 2½" tall. $75.00 – 125.00.

Irregularly shaped pearl face adorns this scarecrow signed "Jeanne" in an oval cartouche. $100.00 – 125.00.

Next, is this a clown or hobo? I'm not sure but this gold-tone fellow with faux pearl accents measures 2½" tall and is unsigned. $75.00 – 125.00.

Lower left: This pearl faced fellow with pearl buttons is signed "Hattie Carnegie" on an oval cartouche. $100.00 – 150.00.

Faux green jade cabochon figures prominently in this scarecrow signed "ERWIN PEARL." An attached paper hang tag notes that this pin was inspired by a piece owned by Jacqueline Kennedy Onassis and sold at Sotheby's in 1996. $100.00 – 150.00.

Faux blue lapis cabochon face is featured in this scarecrow with scarf and hat. Signed "PAULINE RADER." $125.00 – 175.00.

Lower right: The scarecrow with hat and scarf features a faux green jade face. Signed "PAULINE RADER." $125.00 – 175.00.

Bottom: Scarecrow with "straw" and royal blue enameled jacket, pearl face, and top hat is signed "GIOVANNI." $100.00 – 150.00.

Enameled brooch from Vendome features pearl and golden topaz accents. It measures 4" long x 2½" wide. Signed "Vendome" on an oval cartouche. $100.00 – 150.00.

Beautiful rose brooch features pavé-set red and clear rhinestones and red enameling; this contemporary pin is signed "©NOLAN MILLER" on an oval cartouche and measures 2¾" tall x 2¼" wide. Mr. Miller was born in 1935 and began his career as a fashion designer. His fashions first appeared on the June Allyson show. For the next 30 years he continued to design for various television shows including Charlie's Angels, Love Boat, Hotel, Hart to Hart, and Dynasty. In 1992 he began featuring his line of costume jewelry on a popular home shopping network. I love the large and colorful designs which are characteristic of his work. $75.00 – 100.00.

This 1994 brooch was designed by Jose Barrera for Avon. Named "Fashion Flower," the enameled pin features crystal clear rhinestone accents and measures 4½" tall x 3" wide. Signed "BARRERA for AVON." $75.00 – 100.00.

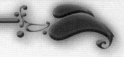

Enormous flower brooches with colorful nylon petals. Each measures 4½" in diameter and are unsigned Hattie Carnegie. $200.00 – 300.00 each.

The pearls and petals on the top of this brooch have been hand-wired to a domed and perforated background. All stones are prong set in this lovely, unsigned brooch. $50.00 – 75.00.

Hang tag and card are intact on this floral brooch set, signed "CORO" on all three pieces. Bright blue enameling is accented by a dramatic black border. $50.00 – 75.00.

Starfish set by Kenneth Jay Lane for Avon features a large center aquamarine stone. The brooch measures 3½" at its widest; the pierced earrings measure 1¼" at widest in this set from the early 1990s. Signed "KJL" on the brooch. $75.00 – 100.00.

Judy Lee set in the colors of fall features watermelon rose-cut chatons in the center of the brooch and earrings. The brooch measures 2¼" in diameter while the earrings measure 1½". All three pieces are signed "Judy Lee" in script with no © symbol. $125.00 – 150.00.

Marvelous lightweight floral set features extended branches accented with aurora borealis chatons. Matching petite earrings and brooch are unsigned; brooch measures 3½" at its widest; earrings are ¾" long. $100.00 – 125.00.

Chatons, pear shaped and marquis diamante, are featured in this dazzling set by Eisenberg. Rows of rhinestone "icing" are shown in the brooch and earrings. All are signed "EISENBERG" in block letters. The brooch measures 3" long x 2" wide; and the earrings measure 1¼" long. $200.00 – 300.00.

The Diamond Look® by Kramer: this lovely "Waltz Time" set was featured in a November 1955 ad from Vogue magazine (see Figure 67). As you can see in the ad, the set incuded a necklace and matching bracelet. Alexandrite in gold finish, signed "KRAMER of New York" on all pieces, including the clip-back earrings. $200.00 – 250.00.

Figure 67: Kramer advertisement featuring the set named "Waltz Time" in Alexandrite in gold finish. A matching bracelet, necklace, brooch and earrings were featured in the ad.

Regency set features stacked flowers with amythest navette petals and aurora borealis centers, all in a japanned setting. Matching earrings are not signed; brooch is signed "REGENCY" on an oval cartouche. $200.00 – 250.00.

Rows of rhinestone icing are featured in this set marked "KRAMER" (only on the earrings; brooch is unsigned). Dogtooth prong settings; brooch measures 2¾" long x almost 2" at widest; clip earrings are 1" long. $200.00 – 250.00.

Layered Juliana brooch with matching earrings features six sapphire oval rose-cut chatons nestled beneath floral rhinestones. Unsigned, the brooch measures 2¾" at its widest; the earrings are 1¼" in length. $200.00 – 250.00.

Striking aurora borealis brooch and matching earrings are signed "SHERMAN," a Canadian company in business from the early 1940s until about 1980. The company made high-quality rhinestone jewelry which was advertised as "Jewels of Elegance." Continental is another Canadian company which often used the same earring backs as Sherman for their higher end jewelry. Some unsigned Sherman jewelry may actually have been made by Continental. In this set, the earrings are signed; the brooch is not. $200.00 – 250.00.

Schreiner demi featuring domed brooch and matching earrings in a japanned setting. This set is unsigned but is definitely Schreiner based on certain design characteristics including open-back setting, japanned setting, and "donut" hole-style clip earring backs. Schreiner jewelry was never mass-produced, increasing its value to collectors. $300.00 – 400.00.

Detail of Schreiner brooch showing its depth; also note on the right-hand side the characteristic donut hole back found on Schreiner earrings.

Married Juliana set features a huge center sapphire stone measuring over 1" long. Open-back setting in shiny rhodium, unsigned. $75.00 – 100.00 for brooch; $25.00 – 40.00 for earrings.
The term "married" is used to denote sets that were not originally made as a set but whose stones and colors match well enough to be worn together.

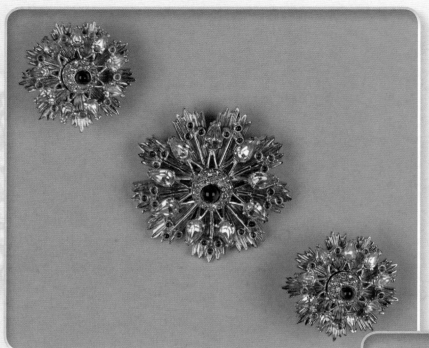

Silver and gold setting features pavé-set crystal clear rhinestones in the center of earrings and brooch; pear shaped diamante provide sparkling accents. The brooch measures 1¾" in diameter; the earrings, 1¼". This well-made set is signed "Nettie Rosenstein." $250.00 – 300.00.

Aurora borealis and black diamond rhinestones are prong set into this atomic-style brooch and matching clip earrings. The brooch measures 3" in diameter; the earrings, 1½". Unsigned. $125.00 – 175.00.

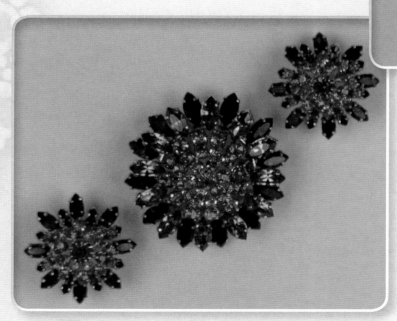

Autumn colored demi from Castlecliff in gold-plated setting; brooch measures 1¾" in diameter; the earrings measure 1¼". Just the earrings are signed on the clips, "CASTLECLIFF." $125.00 – 175.00.

Right: Lovely pink and black color combination is featured in this unsigned stacked brooch which measures 2¼" in diameter; prong settings feature both cupcake (around center chaton) and dog tooth styles. $100.00 – 150.00 for set.

Below: Close-up of matching clip earrings; they each measure 1¼" in diameter.

Left: Starburst brooch with matching earrings set features smoked topaz navettes and aurora borealis chatons; gold-plated setting also features ring support structure characteristic of Juliana jewelry. Brooch measures 3¾" in diameter; earrings measure 1½". $150.00 – 200.00.

Right: Detail of brooch showing the ring support structure found on some Juliana brooches.

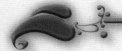

Classic Florenza set features large faux jade cabochons in brooch and earrings. Brooch measures 2" wide x 3" long; earrings measure 1¾" long. All pieces are signed "FLORENZA." $75.00 – 125.00.

Florenza jewelry is very well made and includes Victorian revival themes with antiqued settings and stones that mimic the real thing. Florenza also produced vanity accessory items.

Lovely Juliana brooch measures 3" long, including dangling chain. Matching clip earrings measure 1¼" long. Unsigned. $125.00 – 175.00.

Dangling pearls are featured in a surprisingly lightweight set; the pin measures 3½" long and the clip earrings are 1½" long. The pearls are made of plastic; otherwise the brooch would be very heavy. Unsigned. $50.00 – 75.00.

Popular Castlecliff set designed by Larry Vrba. Mr. Vrba began his jewelry-making career at Miriam Haskell where he worked briefly before leaving with Robert Clark to join William DeLillo. He then joined Castlecliff where he designed this line based on Pre-Columbian and American Indian designs. He later returned to Haskell where he designed the famously popular King Tut series and other bridge jewelry. Today he designs and makes his own jewelry line. Compared to other items in the line, this brooch is rather small and measures 2½" at its widest. Matching screw-back earrings are unusual. All pieces are signed "CASTLECLIFF." $175.00 – 225.00.

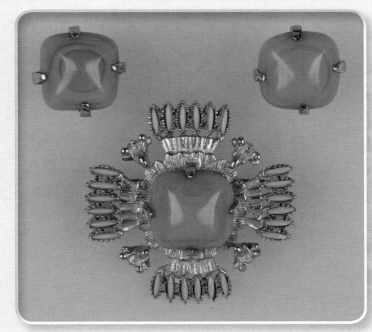

Pell strawberry brooch with matching earrings is accented with emerald rhinestone baguettes in the stems. Just the brooch is signed "PELL." $50.00 – 75.00.

Sarah Coventry 2½" pin from the mid-1960s has matching 1" clip earrings and features ruby red molded glass stones. This set was named "Strawberry Festival." Only the brooch is marked "SARAHCOV©." $50.00 – 75.00.

Popular and collectible "Elephant Walk" set by Elizabeth Taylor for Avon features purple dangling beads; crystal clear rhinestones and gold tassels decorate the elephant with raised tusk for good luck. These sets came packaged in purple felt pouches. Early 1990s. $200.00 – 250.00.

This heavy choker-style necklace features aurora borealis stones and a fish-hook clasp. Unsigned. $50.00 – 75.00.

By the late 1940s cascading necklaces such as the one shown here were becoming popular. They were shown in fashion magazines on models with short hair and dangling earrings. Note the sapphire baguettes providing additional embellishment to the clasp. Unsigned. $50.00 – 75.00.

Gorgeous Donald Stannard necklace with clasp/centerpiece that features tiger heads with ruby red cabochon eyes. The ebony and ivory colored beads are glass; the choker-style necklace measures 16" long. Signed "STANNARD" at the base of each head. $300.00 – 350.00.

Donald Stannard worked briefly for Kenneth Jay Lane before he started his own jewelry line in 1972. He designed many pieces for celebrities, including Ann Miller, who was among his most famous clients.

Stunning double-strand crystal necklace features a gold-plated centerpiece of leaves with dangling "grapes." The drop on the centerpiece measures 3"; the necklace itself measures 14" long. Matching earrings with dangling "grape" crystals are not shown. Only the earrings are marked "Vendome©." $200.00 – 250.00 set.

Black and white bib-style necklace features both plastic and glass beads. Because this necklace is so large, it would be too heavy to wear if all of the beads were glass! The large beads are plastic, made to resemble crackle glass; the smaller clear and black beads are faceted to add sparkle; white enameled beads are sprinkled throughout; each one is set with crystal clear rhinestones. Finally, the black filigree settings add a touch of drama to this magnificent necklace signed "Hobé" on the fishhook clasp. $200.00 – 250.00.

Necklace by Larry Vrba for Castlecliff. This pendant is massive; including the pre-Columbian inspired bail, it measures over 8" long; chain measures 16" long. Signed "CASTLECLIFF." $250.00 – 350.00.

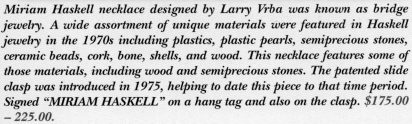

Miriam Haskell necklace designed by Larry Vrba was known as bridge jewelry. A wide assortment of unique materials were featured in Haskell jewelry in the 1970s including plastics, plastic pearls, semiprecious stones, ceramic beads, cork, bone, shells, and wood. This necklace features some of those materials, including wood and semiprecious stones. The patented slide clasp was introduced in 1975, helping to date this piece to that time period. Signed "MIRIAM HASKELL" on a hang tag and also on the clasp. $175.00 – 225.00.

Wide would be an understatement for this bracelet; with emerald and citrine colored rhine-stones, it measures just shy of 3" wide. The larger chatons have dog tooth prong settings. Unsigned. $200.00 – 300.00.

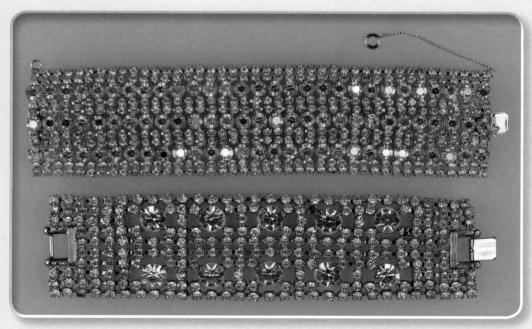

Top: Bracelet measures 1¾" wide, modest by comparison to the bracelet in the former pic-ture! Featuring dozens of prong-set aurora borealis rhinestones, this bracelet is unsigned and measures 7½" long. $175.00 – 225.00.

Bottom: Large diamante chatons accent this bracelet with fold-over clasp. It has no guard chain. Unsigned, it measures 7" long. $175.00 – 225.00.

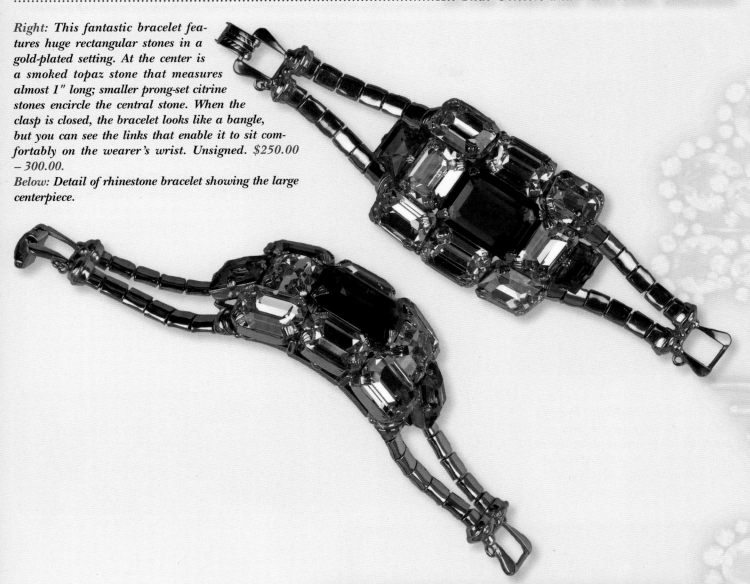

Right: This fantastic bracelet features huge rectangular stones in a gold-plated setting. At the center is a smoked topaz stone that measures almost 1" long; smaller prong-set citrine stones encircle the central stone. When the clasp is closed, the bracelet looks like a bangle, but you can see the links that enable it to sit comfortably on the wearer's wrist. Unsigned. $250.00 – 300.00.

Below: Detail of rhinestone bracelet showing the large centerpiece.

Pretty pearls are featured in a brushed gold-tone setting in this Trifari bracelet which measures 7½" long. It has a narrow fold-over clasp and guard chain. $50.00 – 75.00.

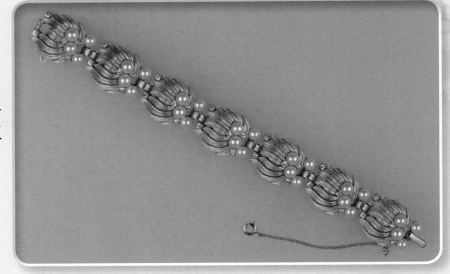

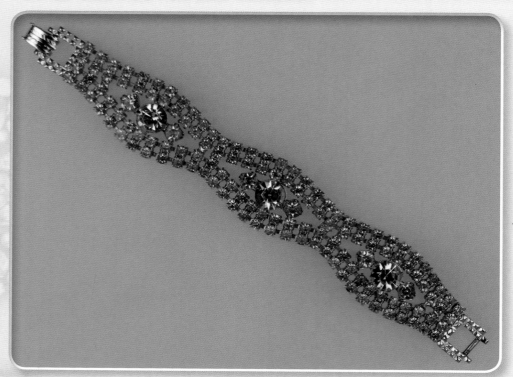

Measuring 1" at its widest, this icy blue rhinestone bracelet measures 7½" long and features a fancy fold-over clasp. $50.00 – 75.00.

Early unsigned Hollycraft bracelet with box chains features a faux jade cabochon center and small enameled flowers in an antiqued gold-tone setting. Unsigned. $200.00 – 300.00.

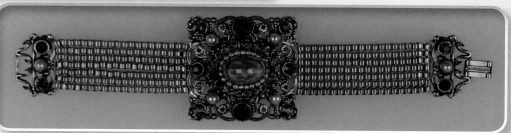

Unsigned aquatic charm bracelet features gold-tone fish with pearls in their mouths and dangling pearl accents. $35.00 – 50.00.

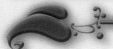

Coro *"Ten Commandments"* charm bracelet is signed "Coro" on the fold-over clasp. The bracelet measures 7½" long; charms measure from 1" to 1½" long. In the late 1950s and early 1960s Coro made many themed charm bracelets. $50.00 – 75.00.

Unusual charm bracelet is made of plastic and glass; the faces are plastic and actually have molded features; the bodies are glass balls with glass rods for legs. Quirky and fun, unsigned, it measures just 6½" long. $100.00 – 150.00.

Ivory and silver Chinese eight-panel bracelet features both male and female characters. Push-in clasp, measures 7½" long, unsigned. $300.00 – 400.00.

This wonderful set features large, polished semiprecious stones throughout; the back of the fancy clasp is signed "JUDITH MCCANN" as is the cross which is mounted in a substantial gold-tone setting. The chain measures 28" long. The cross measures 3" in length; the pierced earrings are unsigned. $150.00 – 200.00.

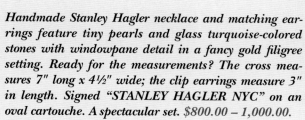

Handmade Stanley Hagler necklace and matching earrings feature tiny pearls and glass turquoise-colored stones with windowpane detail in a fancy gold filigree setting. Ready for the measurements? The cross measures 7" long x 4½" wide; the clip earrings measure 3" in length. Signed "STANLEY HAGLER NYC" on an oval cartouche. A spectacular set. $800.00 – 1,000.00.

Juliana clamper bracelet and matching earrings feature molded iridescent stones and citrine cabochons, all prong set. Unsigned. $150.00 – 200.00.

Popular Juliana set with side-hinge clamper bracelet features pierced faux turquoise inserts and turquoise colored rhinestones. Unsigned. $400.00 – 600.00.

Immensely popular Sarah Coventry set named "Versailles" features large bi-color rose cut center stone; the stones in the earrings are smaller but feature the same cut and colors (olivine and smoked topaz). All pieces are signed. $125.00 – 175.00.

Whiting & Davis demi features genuine mother-of-pearl inserts; similar sets were advertised in the 1976 – 1977 Whiting & Davis catalog; set features bracelet, earrings, and matching ring. All pieces are signed "WHITING & DAVIS Co. MESH BAGS." $75.00 – 125.00.

Spectacular bracelet features six large rectangular shaped stones, each measuring 1" long. Set in shiny rhodium, unsigned, with matching clip-style earrings. $150.00 – 200.00.

Pretty Judy Lee bracelet with matching earrings, this set was named "Rainbow Goddess." The bracelet is signed on the clasp in script, "Judy Lee." All pieces feature a stone named "Irisea" in the original 1965 advertisement.[22] $75.00 – 125.00.

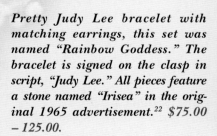

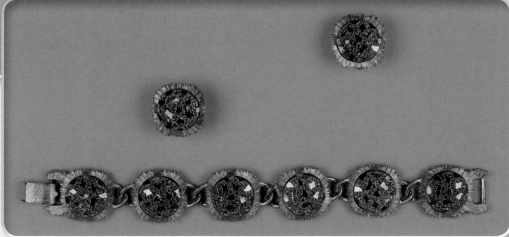

[22] Carroll, Julia. *Collecting Costume Jewelry 303: The flip side, Exploring Costume Jewelry from the Back.* Collector Books, Paducah, KY, 2010, pg. 245.

Vendome beaded set features pearls, filigree balls, and clear crystals in the necklace and matching bracelet. The quality shows in the details; the fold-over clasp on the bracelet is set with baguettes and chatons; the necklace features a fancy floral clasp and also baguettes and chatons. Signed on hang tags, "Vendome©." Matching earrings are not shown. $200.00 – 250.00.

Lilac and pale turquoise beaded necklace by Miriam Haskell features a fancy clasp decorated with fancy filigree flower and crystal clear rhinestones. In the 1970s these beautiful fancy clasps disappeared from the lines. The necklace is heavy and is made of glass beads; signed on the clasp, "MIRIAM HASKELL." $200.00 – 300.00. Coordinating brooch is signed on an oval cartouche, "MIRIAM HASKELL," and has the characteristic gold filigree setting with seed beads and large center bead. It measures 2" in diameter. $200.00 – 300.00.

Bracelet and necklace in white feature aurora borealis chatons interspersed throughout. Unsigned. $100.00 – 150.00.

Sparkling glass crystals are featured in this stunning two-strand necklace with matching earrings. The crystals are wired to the perforated earring components. Unsigned. $100.00 – 150.00.

Lovely Eugene demi features iridescent emerald green glass crystals. The floral centerpiece is enameled with a large emerald crystal center; the earrings cleverly pick up the design of the centerpiece. All pieces are signed. $200.00 – 250.00.

A clever design is featured in this pearl necklace and earring set from Florenza. The necklace can be worn two ways: with or without the looped pearls that you see on top of the choker. They attach under the center pendant. This set was featured in a mid-1960s Sears advertisement. All pieces are signed "FLORENZA©." $150.00 – 200.00.

Above: This Sarah Coventry set is one of the most popular Coventry designs; it features large panel stones which are so called because each large stone creates the appearance of four individual stones. This lovely set was featured in a 1963 promotional advertisement designed to encourage people to join the sales team. The ad noted that in 1962, some 508,000 home shows were held and sold 8,742,449 pieces of Sarah Coventry jewelry. The dark stones are accented with attractive pink chatons. This set includes a matching necklace. A matching ring was also featured (not shown). Unsigned. $100.00 – 150.00 for the set. Right: Matching pendant from Sarah Coventry Midnight Madness set.

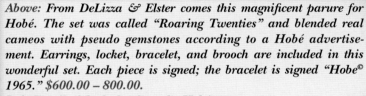

Above: From DeLizza & Elster comes this magnificent parure for Hobé. The set was called "Roaring Twenties" and blended real cameos with pseudo gemstones according to a Hobé advertisement. Earrings, locket, bracelet, and brooch are included in this wonderful set. Each piece is signed; the bracelet is signed "Hobe© 1965." $600.00 – 800.00.

Left: Detail of the locket from the Hobé parure.

Center: Kenneth Jay Lane Duchess Collection features a torsade-style coral colored glass bead necklace. It is a copy of the 18K gold, coral, emerald, and diamond choker made by Cartier for the Duchess in 1949.

Left: The Duchess' beloved pug is depicted in a large pin with pearl body; in the center of the necklace, the coral colored orb is accented with emerald rhinestones and a sparkling butterfly.

Right: The headpiece brooch measures almost 3" tall and is encrusted with crystal clear rhinestones. Fabulous set, all pieces are signed "KJL" on cartouche. $600.00 – 800.00 and up.

Famous Juliana set features the popular heliotrope green margarita stones. The necklace with five dangles was first shown in the design books in 1964. This magnificent set also includes the characteristic five-link bracelet, stylized leaf pin, clip earrings, and the "owl" brooch at the top, nicknamed as such because of its resemblance to an owl. Price for this complete set, $1,200.00 – 1,400.00.

Above: Magnificent Juliana parure featuring rhinestones and beads in a green and purple color combination from the early 1960s. The distinctive aspect of this set is the beautifully made metal filigree ball beads that are used lavishly throughout the cascading necklace, bracelet, and earrings. The filigree beads came in a variety of colors and finishes. $800.00 – 1,000.00.

Left: Close-up of back of Juliana bracelet showing the link construction. In Juliana bracelets there should be five such links.

Popular Juliana set which features the distinctive five-link bracelet and snake chain necklace. Note the rare clasp on the bracelet; each horseshoe-shaped end is covered with tiny rhinestones. Tiny clusters of rhinestones on silver-tone wires overlay the larger stones on both the bracelet and necklace. $300.00 – 400.00.

Intaglio glass cameo parure features necklace, drop earrings, and bangle bracelet; each cameo is surrounded by a silver mesh chain. The set is not signed but resembles sets sold by Whiting & Davis in the mid-1970s. $100.00 – 150.00.
The term "intaglio" means to carve down into a material. Reverse intaglio is done from the back. Materials typically used for reverse intaglio jewelry are crystal, glass, celluloid, or Lucite.

Iridescent Juliana cameo neckace and matching clip earrings are surrounded by smoked topaz chatons and open back navettes. The brooch/pendant was also manufactured by DeLizza and Elster for Celebrity; it is signed "CELEBRITY NY." Necklace and matching earrings, $200.00 – 300.00. Brooch, $125.00 – 175.00.

Copper Jewelry

Francisco Rebajes and Renoir specialized in the manufacture of modernist jewelry designs in copper.

Top: Ubangi brooch, measures 3" tall and is signed. It sold for $2.95 when it first came out. This design was also made in silverplate. $200.00 – 300.00.
Bottom: Brazilian mask brooch was one of Rebajes' most popular creations and was featured on earrings, bracelet, and pendant. Signed. $100.00 – 150.00.

Popular "Leaf" pattern by Matisse/Renoir. The design was featured in a variety of colors, some with copper stud accents like this one. Earrings are signed "Matisse;" brooch is signed "Matisse Renoir©." Brooch and clip earrings, $75.00 – 125.00.

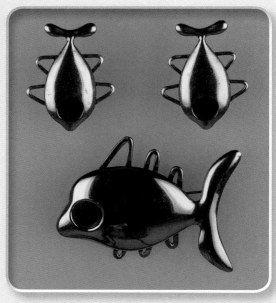

"Corafish" pin and earrings set was only made in copper. Pin measures 2¼" in length; earrings 1½". Signed "Renoir©." $75.00 – 125.00.

Top: "Scarab" earrings feature colorful cabochons. Signed "Matisse," these are part of a matched set that includes a bracelet (not shown). Earrings, $35.00 – 50.00.
Bottom: Set was named "Leaflet" and was one of the most popular made by Matisse/Renoir. It came in other colors including black and white. Clamper bracelet and brooch are signed "Matisse Renoir©" set, $150.00 – 200.00.

Enameled insert is prong set on this copper bangle. Unsigned; however, the clip-back earrings are signed "Matisse." $175.00 – 225.00.

"Sari" design is featured in clip earrings and clamper bracelet. The set also has a matching brooch (not shown). Clip earrings are signed "Renoir © Matisse." $175.00 – 225.00.

Copper link bracelet features confetti Lucite inserts and measures 3½" wide. Unsigned, Selini. $200.00 – 300.00.

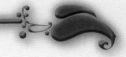

Egyptian Revival

The King Tut exhibit traveled around the U.S. in the early 1970s and resulted in many Egyptian-inspired designs in necklaces, bracelets, earrings, and rings. The Egyptian line from Miriam Haskell was designed by Larry Vrba and it proved to be one of his most popular, lasting from 1972 – 1977. A number of new construction methods were introduced by Haskell in the 1970s including the 1969 patented side clasp which actually appeared on jewelry in 1975. Other companies designed their own Egyptian-inspired lines including Hattie Carnegie and Eisenberg. A perennial favorite among collectors, the popularity of such jewelry transcends the decades. Throughout the twentieth century Egyptian motifs have surfaced again and again in jewelry designs.

Far right: Hattie Carnegie pendant features enameled accents and glass beads. The book chain is accented with turquoise and lapis colored glass beads as well. The pendant measures 4½" long; the chain is 22" long. $300.00 – 400.00.

Right: Detail of Hattie Carnegie pendant showing the signature cartouche.

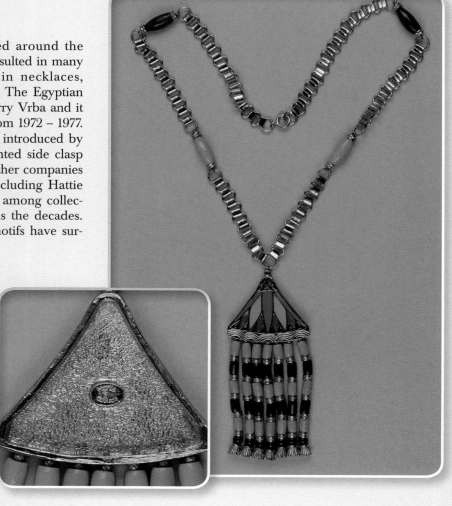

From the popular 1970s line of Eisenberg enameled jewelry comes this Egyptian-inspired necklace. The chain measures 24" long and is marked *"EISENBERG©"* with a hang tag; the pendant is also similarly signed and measures 1¾" x 3" long. $125.00 – 150.00.

Right: Miriam Haskell necklace designed by Larry Vrba. Note the large scarab pendant encircled with faux coral, turquoise, and lapis colored beads. While some plastics were used in this line, the majority of beads are glass. The pendant measures 2½" long; the beaded necklace is 20" long. Signed. $300.00 – 400.00.

Below: Back of Miriam Haskell pendant showing the signature cartouche; note the side clasp and hang tag bearing the Haskell signature.

Scarabs are intended to represent the dung beetle, which the Egyptians held in very high esteem. The symbol represented eternity to them. As such, it figured prominently in their artwork. Precious stones were polished and carved in the configuration of this insect to insure a safe passage into the afterlife.

The Haskell Egyptian line featured bracelets and earrings that could be mixed and matched. Shown here are King Tut earrings and mesh bracelet. The earrings are signed in two places, including on the patented clip-back earrings. The bracelet is signed on an oval cartouche. Earrings, $100.00 – 150.00; bracelet, $175.00 – 225.00.

Left: Although lightweight, this Miriam Haskell necklace and matching bracelet are made with faux turquoise glass beads. The center of both pieces is accented with an image of King Tut. The necklace measures 16" long. In the center is another necklace from the Haskell Egyptian line, this time a pendant on beaded necklace. The pendant is large and measures 2½" in diameter. It is encircled with beads which are wired onto a gilt metal finding. Bracelet and necklace, $500.00 – 700.00. Pendant, $300.00 – 400.00.

Below: Back of pendant detail showing the signature cartouche.

Right: Semiprecious scarabs are set into fancy filigree settings in this 24" necklace from Miriam Haskell.
Below: Matching bracelet and earrings complete the set. All pieces are signed, including the slide clasp on the necklace. The bracelet is signed on the back, "MIRIAM HASKELL" on an oval cartouche. Price for all pieces $400.00 – 600.00.

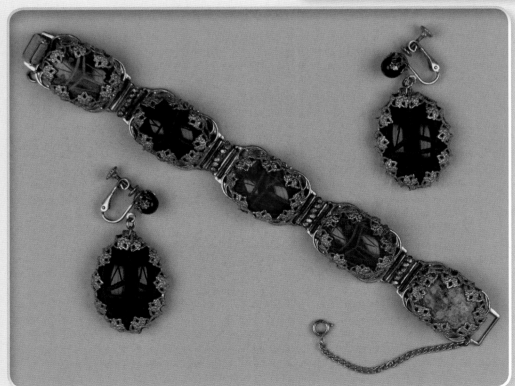

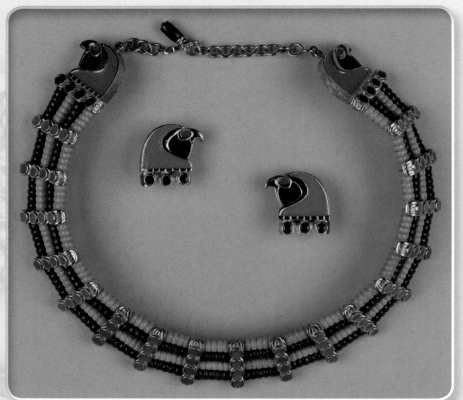

Stunning choker-style necklace from Hattie Carnegie celebrates the rich colors often associated with Egyptian motif jewelry. Here turquoise and lapis colored beads are strung in an alternating pattern and accented with colorful enameling. The earrings match the end pieces on the necklace. All are signed on an oval cartouche, "Hattie©Carnegie." $400.00 – 600.00.

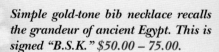

Simple gold-tone bib necklace recalls the grandeur of ancient Egypt. This is signed "B.S.K." $50.00 – 75.00.

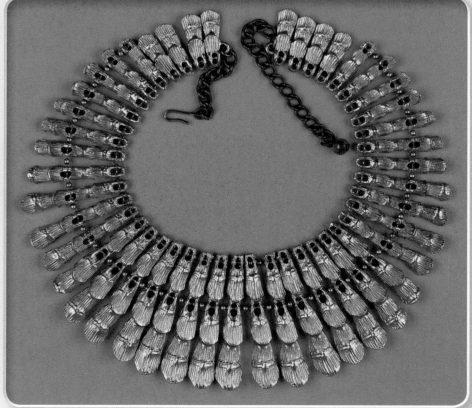

Christmas

These beautiful and massive Christmas tree brooches were made by Eisenberg. Each measures 3" tall x 2½" wide and are set in shiny rhodium with prong-set stones. Eisenberg started making Christmas tree brooches in 1972. Signed "EISENBERG ICE©." $200.00 – 250.00 each.

This beautiful Christmas tree pin was made by Dotty Stringfield (www.illusionjewels.com) and is signed on a disc, "BG." These creations are hand embellished and most are one of a kind. They are made with vintage and contemporary components in distinctive designs. The brooch measures 2" at its widest point and is 4" tall. $150.00 – 200.00.

Six-candle brooch is signed "WEISS" on an oval cartouche. All stones are prong set in this gorgeous favorite of collectors. It measures 2¾ " tall. $175.00 – 225.00.

Left: A colorful Christmas tree brooch features prong-set stones throughout. It measures 3" tall x 2½" at its widest and is set in shiny gold tone. $75.00 – 100.00.
Right: An unsigned beauty with glued-in stones, all shades of green. $50.00 – 75.00.

Left: Japanned setting with both clear and colored stones makes a dramatic impact in this Christmas tree brooch. It measures 2¾" tall x 2½" wide. Unsigned. $50.00 – 75.00.
Right: A festive tree with clear rhinestone garland and green enameling. Signed "JJ©" on a rectangle. $50.00 – 75.00.

Left: A favorite Christmas tree pin by Cadoro. It measures 2⅜" high x 1¾". The partridge is pavé set with clear rhinestones in this version. $75.00 – 100.00.
Right: A fabulous Christmas tree pin signed "MYLU "features irregularly shaped pink stones with rivoli and clear rhinestones. $250.00 – 300.00.

*Left: Pearls adorn this Christmas tree brooch. It measures 1¾" tall x 1½" wide. Unsigned. $35.00 – 50.00.
Right: Another beautiful Christmas tree made by the Eisenberg company. It is signed "EISENBERG ICE©" and measures 2½" tall x 1½" wide. $100.00 – 125.00.*

Remember those bottle-brush trees that were used in gardens under Christmas trees? Here is a bottle-brush Christmas tree brooch with tiny pine cones and red plastic berries. I have never seen another one like it. Unsigned. $45.00 – 60.00.

This is the biggest snowman brooch I have ever seen; he measures over 4" tall. All stones are prong set in this dramatic unsigned piece. $100.00 – 150.00.

Buyer's Table

This section includes an updated list of selected jewelry designers and manufacturers. Dates of operation, signatures, and/or other identifying marks, and typical design characteristics are listed. The table is designed to provide a brief summary for costume jewelry collectors. For more detailed information, please consult the bibliography.

Manufacturer/ Designer	Dates of Operation	Signature/Marks	Description/Characteristics
Art, Mode-Art	1950 – 1980	ART© MODEART	MODE-ART was a New York based company owned by Arthur Pepper. The company marketed to wholesalers a variety of jewelry in a wide range of prices. ART designs cover almost every conceivable design including Victorian revival, whimsical figural jewelry accented with enamel and rhinestones, and Christmas jewelry.
Austria, Made in	Early 1900s – present (most costume jewelry seen in the collectibles market is twentieth century)	AUSTRIA MADE IN AUSTRIA	Jewelry from Austria is well made with top quality rhinestones and some enameling. This jewelry rivals jewelry from the great designers in quality of materials and style. It is readily available in the collectibles market and is generally affordable. Popularity among collectors is increasing.
Avon	1971 – present	©AVON E. Taylor for Avon (1993 – 1997) Barrera for Avon (1989 – 1996) K.J.L. for Avon (1986 – 2005) and at least ten other signatures	Avon was founded by David H. McConnell as California Perfume. The company became Avon Products, Inc. in 1939. After 1971 Avon added costume jewelry to its long list of products. They contracted with existing jewelry manufacturers such as Krementz to produce their jewelry; Avon jewelry includes some very well made designer pieces in a wide range of styles and materials.
Barclay, McClelland	1935 – 1943	McClelland Barclay At least six other signatures were used including Barclay, Barclay STERLING, and Barclay©, used before 1955	McClelland Barclay jewelry is rare and extremely well made; its rarity is due to the fact that Barclay was killed in action in WWII, and thus only designed jewelry for a few years. McClelland designs feature top quality materials in Art Deco designs and the use of sterling silver. Rice-Weiner made the jewelry for McClelland Barclay; this jewelry should not be confused with Barclay, which was founded in 1946 by Alvin Rice, Robert Rice, and Louis Mark in Providence, Rhode Island, after a split with Rice-Weiner.
Beatrix (BJ)	1946 – 1983	BJ BEATRIX	Nat Sugarman started the company in 1946 which he named after his sister Beatrice. In 1965 BJ jewelry was purchased by Leonard Mandell, who was the company's manager. At this time, the company began marketing a variety of Christmas trees and other Christmas jewelry, including their famous Chris mouse pin.
Beau Jewels	1950s – early 1970s	Only earrings are marked "BEAUJEWELS" on an oval cartouche	Beau Jewels jewelry was manufactured by Bowman Foster, Inc. They made large and lightweight rhinestone and beaded jewelry featuring unusual stones (not associated with Beau-craft).
Bogoff	1946 – 1959	BOGOFF Jewels by Bogoff	Bogoff jewelry was made by the Spear Novelty Company. Henry Bogoff and his wife Yvette started the company in the 1920s; at that time the company made accessories. The business was expanded to include jewelry in the mid-1940s and included very high quality rhinestone pieces with a fine jewelry look. Henry died at the age of 50 in 1958; his wife kept the company going for another four to five years. Spear Novelty Company closed in the early 1960s.

Manufacturer/ Designer	Dates of Operation	Signature/Marks	Description/Characteristics
Bonaz, Auguste	Auguste Bonaz was born in 1877 and took over the family business from his father. The Maison Bonaz was active until 1940 despite Bonaz's death in 1922.	Auguste Bonaz	Auguste Bonaz was a well-known French designer who originally made combs in Oyonnax, France. He took over the hair ornament business from his father, Cesar. Bonaz produced horn combs until 1910 and then switched to celluloid for pendants and headdresses. The Maison Bonaz was a great success at the 1925 Exposition des Arts Decoratifs, where they exhibited celluloid combs and dressing table accessories. After women bobbed their hair, Maison Bonaz adapted their product line and produced buckles, buttons, and small figural jewelry. In the early 1930s the company began to make geometric necklaces of Galalith. For more information see *European Designer Jewelry* by Ginger Moro.
Boucher, Marcel Boucher & Cie	1937 – 1971	MB with Phrygian cap (1937 – 1949) BOUCHER (includes inventory number) MARCEL BOUCHER MARBOUX© (Registered in 1937, used in 1955 for less expensive line) BOUCHER with name of flower for flower pins (and at least six other signatures)	Boucher was one of the twentieth century's finest costume jewelry designers. His original and creative designs reflect the technical experience he gained while an apprentice at Cartier. His stylized rhinestone and enameled bird brooches are among his finest work. Excellent quality metalwork with high-quality rhinestones are hallmarks; most jewelry is signed and includes an inventory number. Boucher jewelry is sought after by collectors; some exceptional pieces were included in the landmark "Jewels of Fantasy" exhibit. Some jewelry was designed by his wife Sandra, whose designs were patented.
BSK	1948 – early 1980s	BSK B.S.K. B.S.K. My Fair Lady	BSK was a trademark of B. Steinberg Kaslo, and was owned by partners Julius Steinberg, Morris Kimmelman, Hyman Slovitt, Samuel Friedman, and Arke, Inc. The jewelry features a variety of styles including gold-tone with some enameling and rhinestone accents and well as plastics. The jewelry is reasonably priced and readily available in the collectibles market. Especially popular is BSK jewelry made to coincide with the release of the movie, *My Fair Lady*.
Cadoro	1954 – 1987	CADORO© Nina Ricci for CADORO (1964)	Cadoro was founded in 1954 by Steve Brody and Dan Stonescu. Also involved in the company were Jean-Francoise Herbert and Max Frescoln (as of 1976). The company used only the best materials obtained from European suppliers; their designs were oversized, colorful, and very well made, and often featured excellent quality enameling. Figural three-diminsional fish, animals, and Russian-inspired jewelry is highly collectible. Also very collectible and perhaps best known are Cadoro Christmas tree pins. Dan Stonescu died in 1976; Steve Brody died in 1994. As of 2009, Max Frescoln continues to hold proprietary rights to Cadoro (see Rossbacher, N.D. "Cadoro" in *VFCJ*, Vol. 19, No. 3, 2009).
Capri	1952 – 1977	CAPRI with © after 1955	Capri was owned by Sol Smith. The jewelry was very well made and featured colored rhinestones and pearls in interesting and dimensional designs. Jewelry marked with "CAPRI" without the © was made between 1952 and 1955. Some Capri designs were produced by Florenza.

Manufacturer/ Designer	Dates of Operation	Signature/Marks	Description/Characteristics
Carnegie, Hattie	1918 – 1979	HC in a diamond HATTIE CARNEGIE on an oval cartouche Carnegie Double Exposure (and at least ten others)	Born Henrietta Kanengeiser in Vienna in 1886, Hattie's "rags to riches" life story is remarkable. Her jewelry was originally made to complement her fashions; early pieces included lavalieres, shoe buckles, scarf clips, and hair ornaments. Her highly collectible figural jewelry, which makes liberal use of colorful plastics, includes rams, fish, elephants, Asian themes, and Egyptian Revival designs. She also marketed designs with pearls and rhinestones. Carnegie's first jewelry was made after 1939. In 1976 the company was acquired by Chromalloy American Corp., but the Carnegie name was still being used in 1978. All of her jewelry styles are collectible; her figural jewelry is especially popular with collectors.
Carolee	1972 – present	CAROLEE©	Founded by Carolee Friedlander in 1972, Carolee jewelry is best known for copies of the Duchess of Windsor jewelry, including the famous flamingo pin. Carolee jewelry is well made with high quality materials including faux pearls and clear and colored rhinestones in silver- and gold-tone settings. The Carolee company was purchased by Retail Brand Alliance in 2001.
Castlecliff	1918 – 1977	CASTLECLIFF STERLING CASTLECLIFF CASTLEMARK (1948 – 1952) Anne Klein for Castlecliff (1977)	Castlecliff was founded in 1918 by Clifford Furst and Joseph Babley. They began marketing their jewelry after a court battle with Brier MFG. Co. over design patents. Castlecliff manufactured their own jewelry in New York. In the late 1980s they were bought by Lucien Piccard Industries, which included Pierre Cardin. Castlecliff jewelry is extremely well made using excellent materials, including rhinestones in traditional settings as well as large faux gemstones (faux jade and turquoise) in heavy gold-tone settings. One of the most popular designs ever marketed by Castlecliff includes their American Indian inspired pendants, brooches, and belts designed by Larry Vrba and sold in the early 1970s. The stones featured in this popular jewelry line was made by a company called Jewelry of Four Seasons which Castlecliff owned for about five years.
Caviness, Alice	1945 – 1990s	ALICE CAVINESS on oval cartouche ALICE CAVINESS Sterling Germany ALICE CAVINESS Sterling A.C. with metal content	Caviness jewelry was designed to complement her fashions. Ms. Caviness even had her own jewelry factory. Her business continued after her death in 1983. Her designs are large, bold, and use high-quality materials, including decorative stones. Not all Alice Caviness jewelry was signed.
Ciner	1892 – present First costume jewelry made in 1931	CINER MC on a raised rectangle CINER® (And at least five more)	Ciner features high-quality jewelry that features beautiful designs made with rows of tiny rhinestones, faux turquoise, and pearls, combined with superior metalwork. Only Ciner jewelry produced after WWII is marked. After the Boucher firm was sold, Sandra Boucher worked for a time as a designer for Ciner.
Claudette	1945 – unknown	©CLAUDETTE	Claudette jewelry was made by the Premier Jewelry Company in NYC. Plated jewelry with plastic inserts is more commonly found in the collectibles market, but the company did feature a line of rhinestone jewelry as well.
Continental	1950s – 1960s	CONTINENTAL	Continental is a Canadian company; their well-made jewelry features classic designs with rhinestones and pearls. Their high-end line of rhinestone jewelry is sometimes mistaken for Sherman.

Manufacturer/ Designer	Dates of Operation	Signature/Marks	Description/Characteristics
Coro	1901 – 1979	Coro used many signatures; a few of the more commonly occurring ones are: Coro Coro Craft (1933 – 1979) Corocraft (1945 – 1979) Francois© (1938 – 1950s) Pegasus symbol used after WWII Vendome (see Vendome)	Coro jewelry used approximately 50 different trademarks between 1930 – 1960 but Coro, CoroCraft, and Coro Duette are among the most significant. Emanuel Cohn and Carl Rosenberger opened the Coro factory in Providence, Rhode Island, in 1929 and became the largest manufacturer of affordable and accessible costume jewelry in the U.S. Adolf Katz was a major force behind Coro's designs and the company also employed an outstanding team of designers including Selwyn Young who later joined Lisner; Gene and Reno Verrecchio (Verri), brothers who later founded Gem-Craft; and Anthony Aquilino. Over its long history, Coro jewelry featured a wide variety of designs including figural jewelry with plastic bodies, crowns, beautifully enameled flower brooches, sterling silver retro modern designs, and combination rhinestone/thermoplastic parures.
Craft, Gem-Craft	1948 – present	CRAFT Jewelcraft (the Jewelcraft mark was first used by Coro in 1920; it is now owned by Gem-Craft. They renewed it in 2002.)	Craft is a signature of Gem-Craft which is owned by Ron and Gene Verrecchio (Verri). Gene also designed jewelry for KJL, Capri Mandle, Kramer, Tancer, and Cadoro, and worked as head designer for Coro for over 30 years, with many famous designs to his credit. Gem-Craft jewelry is very well made and features faux pearls, cabochons of faux gems, and enameled designs in gold-tone settings. Gem-Craft was originally called Craftsman. The Jewelcraft mark first used by Coro is now owned by Gem-Craft.
Czechoslovakia	Most of the Czech jewelry in today's collectibles market was made between 1918 and 1938	CZECH Czechoslovakia (two of many marks used)	Costume jewelry made in Czechoslovakia often features distinctive Victorian revival and Art Deco designs. This jewelry is made with high-quality rhinestones, molded and faceted glass beads, and colored glass that was cut to look like real gemstones. Czech jewelry is often marked but in hard to see places, including on a brooch stem or on the side of a catch, the back of a necklace clasp, or on the safety catch. Czech silver jewelry is marked with a woman's head with a scarf or bonnet or a rabbit or goat head (after 1955). Rhinestone jewelry marked "Czech" has recently flooded the collectibles market; the pieces are beautiful but not finished, having either been improperly plated or never plated at all. A quick look at the back of such pieces reveals the poorly finished work.
Dalsheim	1930s – 1978	DALSHEIM White Jet Also identified with hang tags	The company was founded by Maurice Dalsheim in the late 1930s. Most jewelry was not signed and was marked only with a hang tag. Their jewelry was made with seed pearls, glass or plastic beads, and sometimes featured small gold-tone novelty pins, some with enamelwork, in Victorian designs.
DeLizza & Elster	1947 – 1990s 1967 – 1968 designed and sold Juliana line	Juliana jewelry marked with hang tags only "Juliana Original" was used for about two years Other names used included: Mystic Jewelry Greenwood Designs Judy, Judy, Judy Fifth Avenue Accessories	DeLizza & Elster was founded by William DeLizza and Harold Elster in New York City. In 1967 – 1968 D&E designed, produced, and marketed Juliana jewelry (named after Frank DeLizza's mother). However, they mostly made jewelry for others including Weiss, Kramer, Hobé, Eisenberg, and more contemporary companies such as Talbot's and Ann Taylor. Juliana jewelry has distinctive design characteristics, including a five-link design on bracelets, beautiful center stones with open backs, navette rhinestones with unfoiled, open backs, and excellent workmanship. Juliana jewelry is especially popular with collectors and readily available in the collectibles market. The demand for this beautifully made jewelry has caused prices to escalate.

Manufacturer/ Designer	Dates of Operation	Signature/Marks	Description/Characteristics
DeNicola	1957 – 1970	DENICOLA on oval cartouche or raised rectangle	DeNicola jewelry is rare and beautifully made, using high quality materials in oversized and fabulous designs. Jerry DeNicola Inc. of New York marketed this jewelry with the slogan the "real look"; DeNicola figural jewelry is sought after by collectors, especially the popular Zodiac series.
D'Orlan	1957 – present	D'ORLAN©	The company was founded in 1957 by Maurice J. Bradden, a tool and dye maker by profession. Before starting D'Orlan, Mr. Bradden managed a jewelry factory in Belleville, Ontario, for Avon jewelry. Creed Canada purchased all of the remaining products when the company closed its doors in March 2006. According to the website (www.creedcanada.com) Mr. Bradden was associated briefly with Marcel Boucher in NYC in the early 1950s as a protégé of Mr. Boucher. Creed is also the distributor for Lancel and Nina Ricci jewelry.
Eisenberg	1935 – present	EISENBERG (in block letters 1945 – 1958) Eisenberg Original (1935 – 1945) Sterling (1943 – 1948) E in script (1942 – 1945) Eisenberg Ice first used in 1935 Many Eisenberg pieces were unsigned	The company was founded by Jonas Eisenberg in Chicago to sell ready-to-wear fashions. The first Eisenberg jewelry was designed to complement their clothes and was sold as part of the fashion ensemble. These early pieces were unsigned. Jonas' son, Sam, began to sell jewelry separately from their fashions, and by 1958 Eisenberg was out of the fashion business. Made by Fallont Kappel in New York (until the mid-1950s) Eisenberg jewelry is made with high-quality, clear and colored rhinestones in hand settings, including sterling silver. In the 1970s Eisenberg produced a series of enameled jewelry that was influenced by modern artists including Braques, Calder, Chagall, Picasso, and Miró. In 1994 and again in 2000 Eisenberg issued a classic series featuring remakes of their popular designs.
Elzac	1941 – 1947	Not signed, marked with hang tags or labels	Elzac of Hollywood produced large, creative novelty jewelry in the early 1940s using ceramic, Lucite, feathers, wood, felt, and other materials during a period when conventional materials were scarce. The jewelry was made by hand and unsigned, except for a hang tag or label. Designs included animals and exotic faces, some with elaborate headdresses. Several Elzac designs were patented by Elliot Handler.
Eugene	1952 – 1962	Eugene on an oval cartouche	Eugene Schultz made top-quality jewelry of his own design using seed pearls and colored cabochons and crystals in ornate and complex designs. Eugene jewelry was only produced for about ten years as Schultz died in 1964. Sometimes the jewelry is not signed and is somewhat rare in the collectibles market.
Florenza	1950 – 1981	FLORENZA© Used the © before 1955 Rosenfeld for FLORENZA	Dan Kasoff, Inc. first produced jewelry in the 1930s. The Florenza name was first used in 1948. Kasoff started his own company which he named after his wife, Florence. They also manufactured jewelry for other companies including Weiss, Kramer, Coro, Capri, and Estée Lauder. Florenza jewelry is very well made and includes Victorian revival themes with antiqued settings and stones that mimic the real thing. Florenza also produced accessory items.

Manufacturer/ Designer	Dates of Operation	Signature/Marks	Description/Characteristics
Freirich	1900 – 1990	FREIRICH on an oval cartouche; the company began marking jewelry in the 1960s	The company was originally named Maison David and located in both the U.S. and France. It was bought by Solomon Freirich in 1922 and remained Maison David in France but changed its name to Freirich in the U.S. The company made buttons, millinery, and dress ornaments including buttons for Dior and Chanel. Jewelry is generally handmade, excellent quality, and features a Victorian look. Later designs were more varied and included plastics.
Germany, West	1949 – 1990	Made in Germany West Made in West Germany Western Germany Western Germany U.S. Zone Germany (before 1949 or after 1990)	Jewelry made in West Germany is ornate and reminiscent of Victorian designs. It is common to see elaborate filigree settings with cameos, colored cabochons, pearls, and other faux gemstones. It is nicely designed jewelry and is usually moderately priced.
Gerry's	Early 1950s – mid 1990s	GERRY'S©	Gerry's jewelry usually features highly stylized figural jewelry of animals including dogs, cats, and mice. Designs include gold-tone and silver-tone pieces, usually smaller jewelry, using colored rhinestones. It is readily available in the collectibles market.
Goldette	1958 – mid-1970s	GOLDETTE Goldette N.Y.© ©Goldette Goldette®	Goldette is the trademark name of Circle Jewelry Company which was owned by Ben Gartner and son Michael. Well-made Victorian revival styles are hallmarks of Goldette jewelry. They emphasized metalwork with enamel and intaglio accents, and incorporated faux turquoise, pearls, and other imitation stones to provide accents in their designs. Goldette jewelry is not always signed.
Hagler, Stanley	1953 – 1996	Stanley Hagler N.Y.C. Stanley Hagler on an oval cartouche	Stanley Hagler graduated from the University of Denver Law School but went on to create costume jewelry beginning in 1951 in Greenwich Village, New York. By 1968 his breathtaking creations were achieving worldwide recognition and he was recognized by the Great Designs in Costume Jewelry program. His large, bold, hand-wrought designs are sought after by collectors.
HAR	1950s – 1960s	HAR©	HAR jewelry is known for excellent enameling and fantastic figural jewelry; ancient Asian figures with imitation ivory faces, genies, cobras, dragons, and blackamoors; enameled fruit, small whimsical animals, and figures; and very well-made rhinestone jewelry with imitation pearls and iridescent stones. Joseph Heibronner and Edith Levitt founded the company in 1955, just three years after they married. Some of the most sought-after designs, including the dragon and genie pieces, can be dated to April 1959, based on U.S. copyright records. Mr. Heibronner died in August of 1968, which is probably why no records on HAR were found after 1967.
Haskell, Miriam	1926 – present	Early Haskell pieces were not signed; the rarest mark is a horseshoe-shaped plaque bearing her name in capital letters (late 1940s). In the 1950s her name appears on an oval cartouche; also "Miriam Haskell" on an oval hang tag; clasps were also marked.	Miriam Haskell jewelry typically features masses of seed pearls, rich filigree metalwork, and a mixture of beautiful stones. Her jewelry is backed with an openwork plate and was made using the finest materials. Miriam Haskell vintage ads featuring Haskell jewelry are among the finest and most artistic of all vintage jewelry advertisements. Haskell jewelry is extremely popular with collectors. Frank Hess, Robert Clark, Larry Vrba, and Millie Petronzio are notable Haskell designers.

Manufacturer/ Designer	Dates of Operation	Signature/Marks	Description/Characteristics
Hobé	1915 – 1995 Jewelry marked "Hobé" is still being made but the original company founded by the Hobé family is out of business	©Hobé Hobé in a crown Hobé with crossed swords Hobé with metal content Some pieces were dates (1957 – 1965) Several other marks were also used	Begun by Jacques Hobé in Paris in 1887, the company was brought to America by Jacques's son William in 1915. They employed traditional methods when making their unique costume jewelry, which was sold at upscale stores. Hobé is well known for romantic floral brooches and the especially stunning "Jewels of Legendary Splendor" from the 1940s which feature beautiful rhinestones and reverse-carved cameos in elaborate gold-tone settings. Hobé is also known for elaborate and excellently made figural jewelry. William's grandson was running the company when it was sold in 2000.
Hollycraft	1938 – 1971	HOLLYCRAFT COPR. & date (first used around 1950) HOLLYCRAFT COPR. & date (after 1955) Also marked with hang tags Early jewelry was not marked	Joseph Chorbajian emigrated to the U.S. in 1917 where he founded the Hollywood Jewelry Mfg. Company in New York in 1938. The jewelry was known for antique finishes and colorful pastel stones of varying sizes in a variety of beautiful and well-constructed designs. Early Hollycraft jewelry was unmarked; later jewelry was clearly marked with name and date. Signed and dated Hollycraft is sought after by collectors. Hollycraft also made jewelry for Kramer and Weiss.
Hong Kong	1940s – present	HONG KONG	Hong Kong jewelry was made before WWII through the early 1950s and again after the Korean War. It varies in quality; some is above average and some below. Multi-strand necklaces feature fancy clasps with glass, faux pearls, and pretty art beads. Also available in the collectibles market are rhinestone expansion bracelets. Collectors like the plastic fruit and flower necklace and bracelet sets. During the 1980s some of the best fake pearls came from Hong Kong.
Iskin, Harry	1930s – 1953	Cartouche marked with Iskin or logo (Larger capital I intersecting capital H) Mark includes metal content (1/20 12 KGF)	A common theme in Iskin jewelry is floral motifs using Art Deco designs, Victorian revival, and Retro modern styles. Designs include some glass stones, pearls, curlicues, ribbons, leaves, and stamped metal components. Iskin jewelry is somewhat rare in the collectibles market.
Japan	After 1945	Made in Japan (after 1952) Occupied Japan (1945 – 1952)	Jewelry made in Japan is known for the use of inexpensive multi-strand beaded necklaces and matching earrings; also celluloid and some wood figural jewelry featuring a variety of characters, some based on Disney. The celluloid jewelry is gaining popularity in the collectibles market.
Jeanne	1950s – 1960s	JEANNE©	Jewelry marked "Jeanne" features well-made, whimsical figural pieces with rhinestones and beads. Little is known about this mark which is seen infrequently in the collectibles market. I have only seen Jeanne jewelry with the © symbol.
Jonette Jewelry Company	1943 – 2006	J.J. (first used in 1970) Artifacts first used in 1986	J.J. is the mark of Jonette Jewelry Co., founded by Abraham Lisker in 1943 in Providence, Rhode Island. It was first called the Providence Jewelry Company. During WWII they ceased operations and then started again with the name Jonette (name comes from Lisker's parents, John and Etta). They are known mostly for figural pins and Christmas jewelry.

Manufacturer/ Designer	Dates of Operation	Signature/Marks	Description/Characteristics
Joseff of Hollywood	1938 – present	JOSEFF HOLLYWOOD JOSEFF Joseff (recent productions use this mark)	Joseff of Hollywood made historically accurate jewelry for Hollywood films during the 1930s – 1940s. He rented his jewelry to the studios rather than sold it outright; as a result, the company amassed a huge archive from which selected pieces of Joseff jewelry were used again and again in films. In 1937 he started a commercial line which was sold in upscale department stores. His jewelry proved very popular in the 1940s and 1950s and was collected by Joan Crawford, among others. He perfected a finish that did not interfere with the movie set lighting; his jewelry was extremely well made with excellent materials and included both traditional and less conventional subjects. After his untimely death in a plane crash, Joan Castle continued to operate the business. In the 1990s some newly assembled Joseff jewelry designs have been introduced into the collectibles market using older, authentic fittings.
Judy Lee	1949 – 1980s	JUDY LEE Judy Lee Judy Lee Jewels	Judy Lee jewelry was produced by the Blanchette Company based in Chicago and sold through home parties. High-quality designs featured pearls and rhinestones, intaglio cameos, and other interesting stones. Judy Lee jewelry is becoming increasingly popular in the collectibles market, in particular the rhinestone pieces.
Karu	1940 – mid-1970s	Karu KARU Fifth Avenue Karu Arke, Inc KARU ARKE, INC Karu STERLING	Karu was made by Kaufman & Ruderman, Inc. The jewelry featured mostly traditional rhinestone sets similar to Weiss & Kramer; they also made some Victorian revival jewelry. Karu jewelry made during the 1960s has a distinctly "mod" look.
Kenneth J. Lane	1963 – present	K.J.L. KJL Kenneth Jay Lane Kenneth Lane© KJL for Avon KJL for Laguna	Kenneth J. Lane began his career by designing shoes. His jewelry designs were often inspired by his travels and employed a variety of unusual and high-quality materials. He was famous for copying the precious jewels of the rich and famous. His jewelry has employed a myriad of designs over his 40+ year career, from classical to whimsical. His early pieces are especially collectible and command high prices when they can be found. He also designed jewelry for Avon and a home shopping network.
Kramer	1943 – 1980	KRAMER KRAMER OF N.Y. KRAMER of NEW YORK Dior by KRAMER Amourelle (by Frank Hess who joined Kramer sometime after he left Haskell) KRAMER STERLING MADE IN AUSTRIA & KRAMER The Diamond Look	Louis Kramer founded this company in 1943 and was later joined by his brothers Morris and Harry. Kramer jewelry features excellent quality rhinestone jewelry some with "icing" similar to that found on Eisenberg and Weiss jewelry. Louis also designed jewelry which included more casual plastic pieces and pretty enameled designs. The © symbol is not useful in dating jewelry because it was not used after 1955.
Krementz	1866 – 2009	KREMENTZ (did not use ©) Krementz USA At least six other signatures	Krementz was established in 1866. As the market evolved, so too did their products – from collar buttons and cufflinks to finely made costume jewelry in the 1950s. Krementz jewelry employed excellent quality materials. Their signature look is delicate, with the appearance of fine jewelry, because they routinely used 10K and 14K plating when making costume jewelry. Their classic designs changed very little over the years. The company was bought by the Colibri group and closed in 2009 when Colibri went out of business.

Manufacturer/ Designer	Dates of Operation	Signature/Marks	Description/Characteristics
Laguna	1944 – 1980s	LAGUNA KJL for Laguna	Laguna jewelry usually features multi-strand neck-laces with matching earrings. It was made by Royal Crafstmen, Inc. in New York which was founded by Louis and Lillian Detkin. Materials included crystal and plastic beads and pearls.
La Roco	1918 – unknown	Only earrings signed LA ROCO La Roco	La Roco was started by Layko, Ross & Co., Inc. The jewelry was well made, using high-quality materials in distinctive and large gold-tone settings. La Roco jew-elry is rare in the collectibles market; considering its rarity and sturdy construction, it is reasonably priced when it can be found.
Ledo (Polcini)	1911 – 1980s	Ledo (1948 – 1963) In the early 1960s it was renamed POLCINI Lee Menichi for Polcini (1971)	Polcini jewelry was founded by Ralph Polcini and was made by the Leading Jewelry Manufacturing Company. They made high-quality diamante designs and also used some colored stones in beautiful and classic designs.
Les Bernard	1962 – 1996	LES BERNARD LES BERNARD, INC. LES BERNARD STERLING	Les Bernard Jewelry Company was founded by Bernard Shapiro and Lester Joy in 1962. Bernard is the son of Harold Shapiro, who founded the Vogue Jewelry Company. Lester Joy was a designer. Les Bernard manu-factured jewelry which was seen on the television show *Dynasty* and also made jewelry for Mary McFadden, James Galanos, and Ugo Correani. Their jewelry fea-tures very well-made rhinestone pieces in a variety of designs. They also made hand-knotted pearl necklaces. The jewelry is well constructed and of high quality.
Lisner	1904 – mid-1980s	Lisner mark first used in 1938 LISNER LISNER© Lisner And at least nine other marks	The D. Lisner Company was founded in New York in 1904. They did not own their own factory; their jewelry was made by others including Whiting & Davis. Until the 1930s much of Lisner's jewelry was imported from Europe. Lisner imported Schiaparelli jewelry and mar-keted it in the U.S. prior to WWII. In the 1930s Lisner teamed with Urie Mandle (father of Robert Mandle of the R. Mandle Co.) to build a retail, domestically pro-duced jewelry line in Providence, Rhode Island. In the 1970s Richelieu and Lisner became one company and were renamed Lisner-Richelieu. Lisner was acquired in 1979 by Victoria Creations, also known as Victoria & Co. Many Lisner designs feature translucent plastic leaves which may have been imported from Europe. Jewelry produced in the 1950s and 1960s featured timeless designs with leaves, fruits, and flowers. Lisner thermo-plastic parures are extremely popular among collectors. Today the company is owned by the Jones Apparel group.
Marvella	1911 – present	MARVELLA© Marvella And many more	Marvella jewelry was manufactured by Weinreich Brothers Company in Philadelphia, Pennsylvania. They made jewelry for many other companies as well and were probably best known for their well-made faux pearl jewelry. Marvella also made popular figural jewelry and crystal necklaces. In the early 1980s they were purchased by Crystal Brands Jewelry Group, which included Monet and Trifari. In 2000 they were purchased by Liz Claiborne, Inc. Jewelry using the Marvella name is still being produced but manufac-turing has moved out of the U.S.

Manufacturer/ Designer	Dates of Operation	Signature/Marks	Description/Characteristics
Mazer/Jomaz	1926 – early 1980s	MAZER BROS. (1926 – 1951) MAZER (1946 – 1981) JOMAZ (1946 – 1981) MAZER Sterling Also used at least five other marks	In 1923, Joseph Mazer, a Russian immigrant and his brother, Lincoln, founded Mazer Bros. in New York. They began making costume jewelry by 1927; among Mazer master designers was Marcel Boucher. The company consistently used high-quality materials to make well-constructed jewelry. In 1946 the brothers split into Joseph Mazer Co. (Jomaz) and Mazer Bros. Joseph's company was in business until 1981; Lincoln's until 1951. Their timeless and elegant designs are popular with collectors. Jomaz figural jewelry is rare and highly collectible.
McCann, Judith	1955 – 1975	JUDITH McCANN	Judith McCann costume jewelry was first sold in upscale department stores beginning in 1955. A variety of materials was used, including polished semiprecious stones as seen in the examples in this book. In 1975 the company merged with several other companies to form Elle Designs.
Mexico	1940 – present	Mexico 925 (after 1947)	During WWII when costume jewelry materials were in short supply, some companies (including Eisenberg) contracted with Mexican silversmiths to make jewelry. At the same time, jewelry designed and made by Mexican silversmiths also became popular. Much of this jewelry was made in an area of Mexico called Taxco. Since it is still being made and signed "Taxco" and "925," the presence of either of these marks is not necessarily helpful in dating the jewelry. Earlier jewelry has an eagle stamp with a number. Jewelry made after 1979 is marked with the initials of the silversmith and also a number indicating the silversmith's position on a registry.
Mimi di Niscemi	1962 to at least 1985	MIMI d N© date on raised rectangle or cartouche	Mimi di Niscemi is a graduate of the Philadelphia Museum School and School of Applied Arts in Paris. Ms. di Niscemi set up a company in 1962 in New York. She designed and produced jewelry and also established an archive of designs. Her elaborate designs employed pearls, colored cabochons, and rhinestones in interesting and ornate designs. In 1968 she won one of 35 prizes offered by the Great Designers in Costume Jewelry awards sponsored by D. Swarovski. Mimi di Niscemi jewelry is rare in the collectibles market; it is noteworthy for its excellent design, craftsmanship, and materials.
Monet	1929 – present	Monet MONET MONET 2 MONET STERLING Monocraft MONET Jewelers	Monocraft Products, Co. was founded in 1929 by Jay and Michael Chernow in Providence, Rhode Island. By 1937 they were making jewelry sets which were mostly modern gold-tone and silver-tone designs. The company was sold several times and finally acquired by Liz Claiborne, Inc. in 2000.
Mylu	1960s – 1970	MYLU©	Most Mylu jewelry consists of stylized Christmas jewelry and small figural pins. Lynne Gordon and Marge Borofsky founded the company which became a division of Coro in 1968; in the 1970s Lynne and Marge joined Tancer II.
Napier	1875 – 1999	NAPIER name first used in 1922 © used after 1955 NAPIER Sterling Napier And at least 18 others	Napier was founded in 1875 by Whitney & Rice in North Attleboro, Massachusetts. The line includes a wide variety of designs over many years including many classic designs in traditional gold-tone or silver-tone. Napier charm bracelets are highly collectible.

Manufacturer/ Designer	Dates of Operation	Signature/Marks	Description/Characteristics
Pam	Possibly 1950s – 1960s	PAM©	Like many companies of the 1950s – 1960s, little is known about this jewelry. Pam jewelry is of average-quality construction with often striking designs including exotic silver-tone and gold-tone figural pieces with rhinestones. Pam jewelry can also be found in more traditional designs and thermoplastic pieces. It has been suggested that Pam may have been started by a French designer named Pierre Anston Masson, but this information has not been verified.
Panetta	1945 – 1995	©PANETTA	Panetta was started by Benedetto Panetto in Naples, Italy, when he made handcrafted platinum jewelry at his shop. After coming to the U.S., Panetta was the chief model-maker for Trifari, but when they moved to Providence in the 1930s, Panetta stayed in New York City with the Pennino brothers. After WWII he established his own company with his sons Amadeo and Armand. They made original designs hand-set in sterling silver and later worked in white metal using gold and rhodium for a two-tone effect. They were known for the "real look" in fine costume jewelry; their line includes very well-made enameled and rhinestone jewelry. The company continued under the management of Benedetto's sons until it was purchased by a foreign company in the 1980s.
Park Lane, Jewels by	1955 – present	PARKLANE on oval cartouche Jewels by Park Lane (with crown)	The company was founded by Arthur and Shirley Levin in Chicago, Illinois. Park Lane jewelry is sold using direct sales/in-home marketing. They make a variety of above-average pearl and gold-tone jewelry, some featuring rhinestone and/or plastic accents.
Pell	1941 – present	PELL ©PELL	Pell was founded by brothers Bill, Tony, Joe, and Alfred Gaita. Early designs featured mostly clear rhinestones. Pell jewelry is high quality and includes unusual figural pins. Alfred continued in his Brooklyn factory to make tailored gold pieces and gold with pearls. Lucille Tempesta reports that the Pell company is under new ownership and jewelry is still being made in the Long Island City, New York, location for clients including Kenneth Jay Lane.
Polcini (see Ledo)			
Rader, Pauline	1960s – late 1980s	Not signed initially; later jewelry was signed "PAULINE RADER" on an oval cartouche or rectangular hang tag (in the late 1960s)	Pauline Rader's jewelry features big and bold enameled pieces with pre-Columbian, Egyptian, and Greek designs. Her pressed coin necklaces are one of her signature designs. Each year, she presented a cruise line featuring brooches and belts with moveable parts, chains, and giant cabochons in interesting figural jewelry designs. She also designed and sold a men's line including pendants on chains and cufflinks.
Razza, Luca	1958 – present	©L.RAZZA ©RAZZA	Luca Razza began his jewelry career working for Coro. In 1958 he started the Ronnie Jewelry Company with Stanley Conheim. The company made jewelry for Capri, Hattie Carnegie, Coro, Coro of Canada, Kramer, Marvella, and Pakula. With another partner Razza started Donna-Lee manufacturing company and specialized in making key chains. A novel plastics process became the center of new products at Ronnie Jewelry; Razza used plastics in place of metal in rubber molds. The result was a highly-detailed and carved-looking item, many of which were featured in Razza's famous Zodiac series. Certified Corporation bought Ronnie Jewelry in 1970; Luca and Stanley agreed to stay five years (Stanley died in the first year). After five years, Luca left and later formed Plaza Jewelry.

Manufacturer/ Designer	Dates of Operation	Signature/Marks	Description/Characteristics
Rebajes	1932 – 1967	Rebajes Crafts NYC Rebajes Rebajes STERLING	Francisco Rebajes was born in 1906 in the Dominican Republic. He studied briefly in Barcelona, Spain, and then moved to New York in 1923. He eventually became a successful artist and by 1937 his work was recognized at the Paris Exposition Universelle. His upscale New York salon where his jewelry and accent items were sold became a popular meeting place. He eventually returned to Spain where he continued to make jewelry until his death in 1990. His jewelry features mostly modern sculptural designs rendered in copper which have a distinctive look.
Regency	1950 – 1970	REGENCY on oval cartouche REGENCY JEWELS "Fleur de Paris by Regency"	Regency jewelry was made by the Regina Novelty Company of New York. Their jewelry is well designed and beautifully made, using excellent-quality materials and unusual stones. They are particularly well known for their butterfly broches which are considered to be among the best ever made. Regency jewelry is readily available in the collectibles market.
Reinad	1922 – 1950s	Reinad 5th Av N.Y. SCEPTRON (1944) Chanel (1941 – not to be confused with Coco Chanel jewelry) REINAD NYC Reinad	Reinad Fifth Avenue made jewelry for other companies, including Boucher, Carnegie, and Eisenberg. They also featured a retail novelty line named Chanel Novelty Co. which was short-lived because of a conflict with Coco Chanel jewelry, which objected to the use of the name "Chanel." The jewelry that Reinad marketed was excellent quality using classic designs and top-grade materials. It is rare in the collectible market. Jewelry marked "SCEPTRON" features classic 1940s designs and is made using sterling silver.
Reja	1941 – 1953	REJA DEJA REJA STERLING	Reja was founded by Sol Finkelstein. The company began manufacturing jewelry for retail in 1939 under the name Deja, but they were taken to court by DuJay. As a result, they were required to change their name and in January 1941 announced their new name, "Reja." Designs include classic rhinestone brooches and enameled flowers as well as large and beautifully-made figural jewelry. Their elegant designs were offered in boutiques. Not all Reja jewelry was signed.
Renoir Matisse	1946 – 1964	Matisse Renoir Matisse (1952 – 1964) Sateur (1958 – 1963) ©Renoir (and a few others)	Renoir of Hollywood was founded by Jerry Fels in 1946 and was headquartered in Los Angeles. The name was later changed to Renoir of California, Inc. Matisse was founded a few years later in 1952. The company specialized in the manufacture of modernist jewelry designs and brightly colored and enameled copper jewelry brooches, clamper bracelets, earrings, and necklaces.
Richelieu	1911 – 2003	Before 1950s not all jewelry was marked RICHELIEU on raised rectangle Richelieu Bill Smith of Richelieu (1970s)	Joseph H. Beyer & Bros. began producing jewelry with the Richelieu mark in Brooklyn, New York, in 1911. Between 1940 – 1960, they made necklaces and earrings with pearls, enamel pins, and rhinestone jewelry; they also made colorful Lucite sets. Richelieu jewelry is above average to excellent quality with interesting details.

Manufacturer/ Designer	Dates of Operation	Signature/Marks	Description/Characteristics
Robert, Original by	1942 – 1979	Original by Robert Fashioncraft Fashioncraft Robert Robert	Fashioncraft Jewelry Co. was founded in New York City by Robert Levy, David Jaffee, and Irving Landsman. The company was noted for excellent enameling and rhinestone jewelry; it is sometimes confused with Miriam Haskell jewelry as selected pieces employ similar materials and techniques. Around 1960, the name was changed to Robert Originals, Inc. In 1979, the company was named Ellen Designs for Robert Originals (Ellen is the daughter of David Jaffee; she joined the company in 1979). In 1984 the company became Ellen Designs. Today Ellen Wagman sells real estate in New York City.
Rosenstein, Nettie	1935 – 1975	Nettie Rosenstein on raised rectangle STERLING Nettie Rosenstein	Nettie Rosenstein was a fashion designer who made jewelry to complement her fashions. Her well-made jewelry was often made with sterling and rhinestones featuring traditional heraldic symbols. Softer romantic designs, including Victorian styles with cameos, were also made, as was plastic figural jewelry. Nettie Rosenstein jewelry is not often found in the collectibles market.
Sandor	1938 – 1972	SANDOR SANDOR© (after 1954) SANDOR CO.©	Sandor was founded by Sandor Goldberger. The company was known for beaded jewelry with elaborate designs incorporating faux coral, pearls, and crystals (these pieces are rare). More commonly found with the Sandor mark are high-quality enameled pins; Sandor was one of the first companies to feature enameled costume jewelry.
Sarah Coventry	1949 – 1984 also 2002 – 2003	©SARAH ©SARAHCOV SC, SAC, SaC on oval cartouche COVENTRY© and many others	Founded by Charles H. Stuart in 1949 the company was named for Mr. Stuart's granddaughter, Sarah (Stuart also founded Emmons). Coventry jewelry includes a variety of styles and materials and was sold mostly at home parties and given as contestant gifts on game shows. Coventry's excellent marketing strategies helped make Sarah Coventry a household name. Medium to better quality designs run the gamut from Victorian revival to classic and modern designs using rhinestones, gold- and silver-tone, and plastics. Home parties were discontinued in 1984 but started again in the 1990s. The company was sold to a Canadian firm in 1984.
Sceptron (See Reinad)		Sceptron (first used in 1944)	Reinad Novelty Co., Inc. and Sceptron Jewelry Creations formed a partnership resulting in jewelry marked "SCEPTRON." Their retro-modern designs employed excellent-quality materials.
Schiaparelli, Elsa	1931 – 1973 (except for a period of time during WWII)	Early pieces are usually unsigned; may have "SCHIAPARELLI" on raised rectangle. Later pieces are signed "Schiaparelli" on cartouche (after 1949)	Schiaparelli early abstract "arrangements" from the 1930s employed various stones and glass decorations using unconventional materials in outrageous designs. Later Schiaparelli jewelry featured colorful rhinestones in excellent and beautiful designs. The later pieces are not as rare as those produced in France in the 1930s. Schiaparelli jewelry is very popular with collectors. It is both rare and expensive. Unfortunately it has also been reproduced and signed "SCHAPARELLI" (missing the "I").
Schreiner	1939 – 1977	SCHREINER NEW YORK SCHREINER	The company was founded by Henry Schreiner who began his career in the 1920s with a company that manufactured shoe buckles. Schreiner jewelry was never mass produced. Intricate, expertly crafted designs with characteristic use of rhinestones (inverted) often in japanned settings have helped make Schreiner jewelry popular with collectors. Early pieces were unsigned but informed collectors are able to identify Schreiner jewelry by looking for characteristics design features.

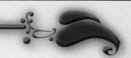

Manufacturer/ Designer	Dates of Operation	Signature/Marks	Description/Characteristics
Selini	1950s – 1970s	SELINI© on raised rectangle; some jewelry is marked with both names (Selro & Selini) Selini jewelry is not always marked; some pieces were marked with hang tags	Paul Selenger formed the company and named it after his mother Rose; Selro was first, then Selini in an attempt to differentiate the two. While Selini is best known for figural jewelry, including Asian and devil face designs, it also featured excellent quality classic rhinestone designs with enameled accents. Collectors love the figural jewelry as well as the more traditional designs. Unsigned pieces can be identified by their her-ringbone chains on the lariat necklaces and elaborate metal settings.
Selro	1950s – 1970s	SELRO CORP© on raised rectangle	See Selini above: best known for figural jewelry, Asian and devil faces; it is extremely well made, highly col-lectible, and not always signed. The company also pro-duced excellent quality rhinestone jewelry. The jewelry was made in New York City.
Sherman	1940 – 1981	SHERMAN SHERMAN STERLING Sherman	Sherman is a Canadian company which made beautiful and high-quality rhinestone jewelry. Their jewelry, which was advertised as "Jewels of Elegance," can be found in the collectibles market and often fea-tures aurora borealis rhinestones in various shapes, including navettes which are most commonly seen. Continental is another Canadian company which used, in their top line, the same earring backs as Sherman. Some unsigned Sherman jewelry may actually have been made by Continental.
Silson	1937 – 1940s	Lacette (first used in March, 1941) Wings of Glory SILSON SILSON PAT PEND on oval cartouche	Silson was founded in New York in 1937 by brothers Victor and Jack Siberfeld, who later changed their name to Silson. The company was best known for patriotic jewelry; they also made fantasitic figural jew-elry and many of their designs were patented. They made limited edition brooches in crystal and vermeil.
Simpson, Adele	1940s – 1950s	Adele Simpson on raised rectangle	Adele Simpson was a fashion designer who produced jewelry to coordinate with her couture line. Jewelry was produced in limited quantities and was expensive when it was first marketed. It is rare in the collect-ibles market.
Sleeper, Martha	1930s	Martha Sleeper jewelry was not signed	Martha Sleeper was born on 6/24/1910 and became a movie and stage actress, starring in a series of films and silent *Our Gang* shorts. Her last movie was *The Bells of St. Mary's* in 1945. By 1949 she was out of the acting business and first settled in Puerto Rico, then South Carolina, where she died in 1983. During the late 1930s, Ms. Sleeper made jewelry from wood and plastic (Bakelite) while living in California. Her style was quirky and in perfect tune with the novelty jew-elry of the 1930s. She made jewelry ducks, cactus, grasshoppers, palm trees, pineapples, squirrels, pup-pies, fish, and lizards, among other things. Her signa-ture style is easily recognized in her jewelry and it is highly collectible.
Spinx	1950 – present	SPINX with design number or the number only	Spinx is a British firm founded in 1950 by S. Roat in Chiswick. Spinx has made jewelry for K.J.L., Butler & Wilson, 5th Avenue, and others. It is well made and somewhat rare in the collectibles market.

Manufacturer/ Designer	Dates of Operation	Signature/Marks	Description/Characteristics
Stannard, Donald	1968 – present	©DONALD STANNARD	Donald Stannard was Kenneth J. Lane's assistant from 1968 to 1972, at which time he started his own line. He made jewelry for Broadway shows including *Panama Hattie, Anything Goes, Pal Joey, Evita, Hello Dolly, On the Twentieth Century, Annie,* and *A Little Night Music.* His jewelry was also featured on television shows including *Dynasty, All My Children,* and *One Life to Live.* Stannard made unique jewelry for Hollywood clients including Ann Miller, Arlene Dahl, Carol Channing, Mary Martin, Ethel Merman, Ruth Warrick, Loretta Young, Ginger Rogers, Dixie Carter, Phyllis Diller, Audrey Meadows, Jayne Meadows, Jane Powell, Elaine Stritch, and The Erte Collection. He currently designs jewelry for individuals. His jewelry is extremely well made, using high-quality materials in ornate settings.
Star	1940s – 1960	STAR	Little is known about jewelry marked "Star." It often featured typical mid-century plastic designs incorporating metal fittings with thermoplastic inserts. Star also marketed some rhinestone figural jewelry.
Star-Art	1940s (perhaps earlier) – 1960s	STAR-ART mark includes metal content	There is no reliable information on Star-Art jewelry. The designs that are found in the collectibles market feature delicate floral designs in retro-modern styles with curled metal and some rhinestones.
Staret	1940 – 1947	STARET	Staret was located at 322 S. Franklin in Chicago, Illinois. Staret jewelry features large settings with enameled pot metal in fabulous designs, including the famous Liberty Torch brooch. It has been reported that they were in some way aligned with the Eisenberg company, perhaps due to the similarity of some designs, but this is not true. Little is known about the company other than they produced some of the most collectible costume jewelry ever made.
St. Gielar, Ian	1989 – present	STANLEY HAGLER NYC on an oval cartouche Ian St Gielar on an oval cartouche (both signatures are on each piece)	Ian St. Gielar jewelry was individually made and each item signed and numbered. Production was limited to six items per design. The beautiful and colorful contemporary designs employed a variety of materials and show the influence of Miriam Haskell and Stanley Hagler. St. Gielar's wife is continuing to make jewelry in his style, following Ian's untimely death in 2007.
Swarovski	1895 – present	S.A. SAWY Swan mark	In 1892 Daniel Swarovski invented a machine that could cut crystals. Daniel, brother-in-law Franz Weis, and Armand Kosmann founded Swarovski in 1895. Swarovski began making its own jewelry line in the late 1970s. As of January 2006 most production was in Asia and Europe. The company now sells through its own line of retail shops. Swarovksi jewelry is excellent quality in classic designs in gold-tone and silver-tone featuring clear and colored rhinestones.
Tara	1960s	TARA	Tara jewelry was sold at home parties. It features colored rhinestones in gold-tone settings and rhinestones in thermoplastic jewelry designs. Tara Fifth Avenue jewelry moved from New York to California in the mid-1960s.
Taylord	1940 – unknown	TAYLORD 1/20 12K GOLDFILLED TAYLORD STERLING	Taylord jewelry was made in Newark, New Jersey. Their designs are typically retro modern.

Manufacturer/ Designer	Dates of Operation	Signature/Marks	Description/Characteristics
Trifari	1918 – present	There are many different marks for Trifari jewelry; the most commonly seen is TRIFARI© with a small crown over the "T." See *Collecting Costume Jewelry 101* by Julia Carroll (Collector Books) for a more complete list of Trifari marks.	Trifari made jewelry beginning in the mid-nineteenth century in Italy. Gustavo then came to the U.S. in the early part of the twentieth century and after serving as a jewelry apprentice, he established Trifari costume jewelry. It was short-lived however, lasting just two years. In 1917 Loe Krussman joined Trifari; by 1925, Trifari, Krussman, and Fishel was established. Alfred Phillipe joined Trifari as chief designer in 1930 after having designed jewelry for Cartier. Trifari's brilliant marketing campaign, beginning in 1938, helped make it a household name. Philippe's original designs helped cement Trifari's reputation. Trifair jewelry features a wide variety of beautiful and unique designs employing rhinestones, enamel, plastics, faux gemstones, and pearls. Their sterling silver crowns and "jelly belly" brooches are among the most famous and collectible of Trifari designs.
Van Dell	1938 – 2009	VAN DELL STERLING VAN DELL with metal content	Van Dell Corporation was established in Providence, Rhode Island, in 1939. Designs feature floral, rhinestones, enameled pieces, and hand-carved ivory. It was sold to Colibri in 1991 who also purchased Krementz. Colibri closed its doors in 2009.
Vendome (Coro)	1944 – 1970	VENDOME VENDOME©	Coro's high-end line of jewelry (CoroCraft) was replaced by Vendome. The chief designer of Vendome jewelry was Helen Marion, whose designs feature high-quality rhinestones and beads, rich enameling, and excellent metalwork. Beaded necklace demi parures are more common in the collectibles market than the elaborate enameled jewelry.
Vogue	1936 – 1975	VOGUE VOGUE STERLING Vogue Jlry	Vogue was founded by Harold Shapiro, Jack Gilbert, and George Grand. Their designs feature some figural pins as well as the more commonly found beaded jewelry. Earlier Vogue pieces, from the 1930s and 1940s, are rarely found in the collectibles market.
Vrba, Larry	1969 – present	LAWRENCE VRBA LTD LAWRENCE VRBA on a cartouche	Larry Vrba began his 40+ jewelry-making career at Miriam Haskell where he worked briefly before leaving with Robert Clark to join William DeLillo. He then joined Castlecliff, where he designed a popular line based on pre-Columbian and Native American designs, inspired by jewelry he found at the Museum of Natural History in New York City. In 1973 he rejoined Haskell as head designer where he worked until 1981. At Miriam Haskell he designed the popular King Tut series which was extremely well received and stayed in the line for five years (1972 – 1977) due to its popularity. He then worked briefly for Les Bernard and in 1983, Mr. Vrba began designing and making his own jewelry line. Today he continues to make jewelry using beads and rhinestones from his vast collection. His jewelry, oversized and dramatic, has been made for the Broadway stage, boutiques, and vintage jewelry shops.
Warner	1953 – 1971	WARNER on oval cartouche	Warner was founded and operated by Joseph Warner. The jewelry was made with colorful rhinestones, in outstanding floral, fruit, and insect designs. Japanned settings helped give Warner its distinctive look. It is very well made using excellent materials and is somewhat rare in the collectibles market.

Manufacturer/ Designer	Dates of Operation	Signature/Marks	Description/Characteristics
Weiss	1942 – 1971	WEISSCO (first used in 1947) WEISS with © after 1955 A.W. Co with a large center "W" in the shape of a crown Jewelry was also marked with hang tags	Albert Weiss founded the company in 1942 and also designed jewelry, having gained experience in the field when he worked for Coro. Michael Weiss continued to operate the company after his father's death until it ceased operations in 1971. Weiss designs include beautiful clear and colored rhinestone jewelry in gold-tone, silver-tone and japanned settings, plastic jewelry including fabulous colored plastic and rhinestone clamper bracelets, and enameled pieces, including some Christmas and flower jewelry. Weiss black diamond jewelry features smoky quartz-colored rhinestones in lovely and classic designs. Weiss jewelry is well made and available in the collectibles market. It is also possible to find Weiss vintage ads which help to identify and date jewelry. Unfortunately Weiss jewelry has been reproduced and is being sold on eBay and elsewhere. The copies are attractive but can be identified by looking at the backs – the fakes have a textured finish while authentic pieces have smooth finishes.
Whiting & Davis	1926 – 1991 They stopped producing non-mesh jewelry in 1980 and all jewelry in 1991.	Whiting & Davis Co. Bags	C.W. Whiting worked for a chain manufacturing company which was founded in 1876. He later became part owner and the company began producing jewelry in 1907. Whiting & Davis was best known for their mesh bags but they also made excellent quality museum jewelry reproductions. Made in the 1950s, these sets are extremely popular with collectors. Their mesh evening bags continue to be popular with collectors.
Wiesner	1953 and perhaps earlier	JOSEPH WIESNER N.Y. on oval cartouche some jewelry is marked "WIESNER" but it is not certain what company made this jewelry	Joseph Wiesner jewelry features beautiful and well-made clear and colored rhinestone jewelry, some featuring Art Deco designs. The 1960 *Jewelers Buyer's Guide* provides an address for Joseph Wiesner on 16 W. 37th Street in New York City. Joseph Wiesner jewelry is somewhat rare in the collectibles market.

Bibliography

Baker, Lillian, *Plastic Jewelry of the Twentieth Century*. Collector Books, Paducah, KY, 2003.

Ball, Joanne Dubbs. *Jewelry of the Stars: Creations from Joseff of Hollywood*. Schiffer Publishing Ltd., Atglen, PA, 1991.

Becker, Vivienne. *Fabulous Costume Jewelry: History of Fantasy and Fashion in Jewels*. Schiffer Publishing Ltd., Atglen, PA, 1993.

Brunialti, Carla Ginelli and Roberto Brunialti. *American Costume Jewelry, Art and Industry, 1935 – 1950, A-M*. Schiffer Publishing Ltd., Atglen, PA, 2008.

Burkholz, Matthew L. and Linda Lichtenberg Kaplan. *Copper Art Jewelry: A Different Lustre*. Schiffer Publishing, Ltd., Atglen, PA, 1992.

Carroll, Julia C. *Collecting Costume Jewelry 202: The Basics of Dating Jewelry, 1935 – 1980*. Collector Books, Paducah, KY, 2007.

Cera, Deanna Farretti, ed. *Jewels of Fantasy*. Harry N. Abrams, Inc., New York, NY, 1992.

DiNoto, Andrea. *Art Plastic: Designed for Living*. Cross River Press, Ltd., New York, NY, 1984.

Duffy, Clinton T. "I'm Going Stir Crazy Warden!" *Saturday Evening Post*, April 29, 1950.

Eytel, Lola. *The Hummel-Book*. Emil Fink Verlag Stuttgart, Germany, 1934.

Fenichell, Stephen. *Plastic: The Making of A Synthetic Century*. Harper Collins, New York, NY, 1996.

Flood, Kathy. *Costume Jewelry Figurals*. Krause Publications, Iola, WI, 2007.

Galas, Judith C. *Plastics: Molding the Past, Shaping the Future*. Lucent Boos, San Diego, CA, 1995.

Gordon, Cathy and Sheila Pamfiloff. *Miriam Haskell Jewelry*. Schiffer Publishing Ltd., Atglen, PA, 2004.

Hellum, Amanda Watkins and Franklin H. Gottshall. *You Can Whittle and Carve*. Bruce Publishing Company, Milwaukee, WI, 1942.

Izard, Mary Jo. *Wooden Jewelry and Novelties*. Schiffer Publishing Ltd., Atglen, PA, 1998.

Jewelers' Buyers Guide 1960, A. McKernin Publication, issued August 1959.

Jewelry Men Told to End Metal Use. *New York Times*, March 25, 1942.

Just, Judith. *Lea Stein Jewelry*. Schiffer Publishing, Ltd., Atglen, PA, 2001.

Kelly, Lyngerda and Nancy Schiffer. *Plastic Jewelry* 4th edition. Schiffer Publishing, Ltd., Atglen, PA, 2001.

Klein, Susan Maxine. *Mid-Century Plastic Jewelry*. Schiffer Publishing Ltd., Atglen, PA, 2005.

Lane, Kenneth Jay and *Harrice Simmons* Miller. *Faking It*. Harry N. Abrams, Inc., New York, NY, 1996.

Lauer, Keith and Julie Robinson. *Celluloid: Collector's Reference and Value Guide*. Collector Books, Paducah, KY, 1999.

Leshner, Leigh. *Collecting Art Plastic Jewelry*. Krause Publications, Iola, WI, 2005.

Moro, Ginger. *European Designer Jewelry*. Schiffer Publishing Ltd., Atglen, PA, 1995.

Mulvagh, Jane. *Costume Jewelry in Vogue*. Conde Nast Publications, Ltd., New York, 1988.

Parry, Karima. *Bakelite Pins*. Schiffer Publishing Ltd., Atglen, PA, 2001.

Patterson, Dick. "Memories of World War II." *Historical News*, Adams County Historical Society, Hastings, NE, Volume 28, No. 4, 1995.

Pinch of War Felt in Novelty Exhibit. *New York Times*, February 5, 1942.

Pitman, Ann Mitchell. *Inside the Jewelry Box*. Collector Books, Paducah, KY, 2004.

Pitman, Ann Mitchell. *Inside the Jewelry Box, Volume 3*. Collector Books, Paducah, KY, 2009.

Rehmann, Jacqueline. *Classic American Costume Jewelry*. Collector Books, Paducah, KY, 2009.

Reinitz, Bertram. "Now Our Jewels are Synthetic: Stones, Glass and Compositions of Metal Are Imported by American Manufacturing Jewelers and Turned Into Trinkets of Odd Styles." *New York Times*, January 27, 1929.

Rezazadeh, Fred. *Costume Jewelry – A Practical Handbook and Value Guide*. Collectors Books, Paducah, KY, 1998 (values updated 2006).

Shields, Jody. *All That Glitters*. Rizzoli International Publications, New York, 1987.

Tolkien, Tracy and Henrietta Wilkinson. *A Collector's Guide to Costume Jewelry: Key Styles and How to Recognize Them*. Firefly Books, Canada, 1997.

www.illusionjewels.com

www.hattie-carnegie.com

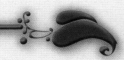

Index